WHAT ARE PEOPLE SAYING ABOUT
GET OFF YOUR ATTITUDE?

"Your ability to be positive and constructive toward yourself, your experiences, and your future can change your life—and this book shows you how to do it."

Brian Tracy
Author, *Million Dollar Habits*

"Packed with dynamic, life-changing ideas, *Get Off Your Attitude* is a must read! Through powerfully motivating and inspiring stories, insightful strategies, and straight-forward advice guaranteed to produce results, Ryan Lowe will take you to new heights of fulfillment and success in life by empowering you to improve your attitude."

Dr. Ivan Misner
NY Times Bestselling Author
Founder of BNI® and Referral Institute®

The philosophy Ryan Lowe shares in *Get Off Your Attitude* is life-changing! Read this book, put Ryan's tips into practice and begin to see a breakthrough in your life!"

Michelle Prince
Best-Selling Author, *Winning In Life Now*
www.WinningInLifeNow.com

"This book goes right to the heart about the importance of attitude and the reasons why individuals have a difficult time achieving a positive attitude. Ryan provides insights into the challenges we all face, and then gives practical solutions so we can achieve a level of awareness that will result in a happier, healthier life. Enjoy the journey and *Get off Your Attitude!*"

Jim Monk, Cofounder
Creating Yourself at the Top
www.creatingyourselfatthetop.com

"I am a big believer that a positive attitude and belief in oneself is the key to reaching your dreams. This book, *Get Off Your Attitude,* will not only explain the important keys of reaching your dreams, but it will also give you the steps to achieving them."

Ruben Gonzalez
Olympian, Business Author, Speaker
www.OlympicMotivation.com

"Ryan's *Get Off Your Attitude* message personally inspires me to be conscious of my daily attitude and encourages me to embrace one of the greatest gifts God has given me as a leader—the power to choose a positive attitude in life!"

Gary J. Borgstede
President & Founder
The Make It Happen Learning Institute
www.makeithappenlearninginstitute.com

"Ryan Lowe and his new 'more than a book, but a life strategy' *Get Off Your Attitude* teaches you not only the importance, but also the steps it takes to master the art of getting out of your own way. GOYA is a great blueprint for success for anyone who either needs a kick in the butt or a fresh reminder of how to live your life each and every day. You really do have a choice. Learn from the best! Thank you, Ryan. I'm proud to know you and learn from you!"

Erik E. Swanson
Habits Success Coach
Author of *HABITUDES*
www.newhabitudes.com

"In *Get Off Your Attitude,* Ryan reveals those qualities by captivating you with gripping conversations called stories from his own experiences and then he connects the dots by showing you just how powerfully important it is to maintain a positive attitude. This book has substance, enlightenment and value, three things all great books possess. I predict that GOYA will be a must read for generations to come. Thanks Ryan, for producing such a remarkable piece of work."

Larry D. Patton
Self-Improvement Expert
Creator of the Laser FOCUS Success System
www.larrydpatton.net

"Whether you're facing challenges in your career, finances, spirituality, health, or something personal, Ryan Lowe's book, *Get Off Your Attitude,* touches the foundation of what bad habits lead to depression and what mindset it takes to overcome those negative thoughts. I recommend Ryan's book to people facing obstacles who want to change their current mindset and start living happier, healthier lives."

George Baehr
President, iTrack Networks, Inc.
www.itracknetworks.com

"Marvelous Performance will not occur for you without embracing Ryan Lowe's nuggets of wisdom. Just his 'GOYA-cises' alone will catapult you to the next level."

Marvin LeBlanc, LUTCF, CNP
Author, *Come Hell or High Water*

"Ryan has achieved excellence in his first writing endeavor. The insights and real-world experience that

Ryan shares are compelling, meaningful, and absolutely right on target in today's world. In a concise and candid approach, Ryan teaches how we can all 'Soar with the Eagles' and realize that our dreams are within our reach if we go after them.

"I would highly recommend that you pick up a copy of *Get Off Your Attitude* and begin making positive choices in your life!"

Chris Brock
Senior Business Development Consultant
RE/MAX Mid-States & Dixie Region

GET OFF YOUR
ATTITUDE

GET OFF YOUR
ATTITUDE

Change *your* Attitude
Change *your* Life

RYAN C. LOWE

sound wisdom
Shippensburg, PA

Sound Wisdom
167 Walnut Bottom Road
Shippensburg, PA 17257

Reach us on the Internet: www.soundwisdom.com

This book and all other Sound Wisdom books are available at bookstores and distributors worldwide.

ISBN 13 TP: 978-0-7684-1302-1
ISBN 13 Ebook: 978-0-7684-8702-2

For Worldwide Distribution, Printed in the U.S.A.

5 6 7 8 / 15 14 13 12

DEDICATION

This book is dedicated to my Grandmother, Violet Lulei Ahten (1919-1988). She (Maw Maw) left an amazing and lasting impression on me. She played a special role in that short period of time… my childhood, my coming of age. Her words of wisdom, her compassion and devotion to those she loved, and the ways she made me feel loved, I will pass along to future generations. I love her and miss her every day. She is my guardian angel.

CONTENTS

Foreword by Julio Melara............................ xv

Acknowledgments xvii

Introduction xxi

Chapter 1   Choose to Be Positive............................1

Chapter 2   Soar With the Eagles 17

Chapter 3   Dream Out Loud............................27

Chapter 4   Get on With It............................ 47

Chapter 5   Get Past Your Past............................59

Chapter 6   Just Smile............................ 67

Chapter 7   Act in Faith............................ 79

Chapter 8   Have a Wealth of Health............................93

Chapter 9   Make Money, Do Good............................ 105

Chapter 10   Say Thank You............................ 119

Chapter 11   Be Someone's Miracle 127

Chapter 12   Make It Happen!............................ 135

Meet the Author 147

Foreword

Success—everyone is searching for it. There are so many elements that are important in order to grow, flourish, and succeed in life. However the foundation for success is built on learning from all different types of people and sources. A few years ago, I met Ryan Lowe and then invited him to come speak to our sales team. I knew there was something different about him. His energy, smile, and confidence certainly radiated. His enthusiasm was contagious too. But the thing that stood out most was his *attitude*. I loved his positive attitude because I believe having the right attitude in life is what separates winners from losers—those who want to be successful from those who are successful.

Many of us have heard speakers say, "Attitude is everything," but they were wrong. Dead wrong. You can have the right attitude or a positive attitude, but if you are incompetent, you will lose in any arena of life. The truth is that while attitude is not everything it is the *most important thing in your life*. Think about it. Your attitude not only affects who you are today, but it also directs your future. Your attitude determines your actions, and your actions determine your achievements. If I could share only one thing I possess, it would be my attitude. My attitude, more than anything else, has helped me on my success journey. That is why I love *Get Off Your Attitude*. Inside this book, you'll discover Ryan's key to developing and maintaining a positive attitude regardless of what happens in life. You'll learn how to let go of the past, get rid of negative voices in your head and grow to your full potential. Today I challenge you to read the entire book, and read it with a highlighter to go back and re-read those areas you want to focus on. Reading this book will help you become stronger, healthier, and stay younger. After all, it's not your age that counts, it's your attitude!

Julio Melara
Publisher, 225 magazine
Author of *It Only Takes Everything You've Got!*

ACKNOWLEDGMENTS

I thank God for giving me such a great family, friends and the talents I needed to make this dream come true. I believe He gave me these four special words, "Get off Your Attitude." These four words, these gifts, have changed my life forever!

As with any dream, I could not have accomplished it alone. A team of very special people helped me bring it to life. They are my "eagles." My sincere thanks go out to them:

Ann Marie Lucito – for your love, loyalty and support. You make me strive to be a better person every day. I love you. You are amazing!

To my mother, Diane "Dee" Lowe, and my father, Aurelius "Butsie" Lowe – for teaching me to persevere. Thank you for being an extraordinary example of what happens when you commit to something great. I love you very much!

To my handsome nephews and my beautiful niece - for sharing your smiles and for bringing such great joy into my life. You are wonderful!

To the rest of my family– to the ones who know me the best, I appreciate your unconditional love, encouragement and support.

Jim Monk – for your belief in me and for sticking by me since day one. I treasure your advice, friendship and encouraging words.

Craig Marinello – for taking the time to assist me and for being a great coach. You were the catalyst to this project.

Julio Melara - for sharing your wisdom and for being a great mentor and friend.

Amber Jensen –for planting the seed of "faith" in me and for giving me the vision for my journey.

George Baehr – for your support, words of encouragement and your great advice.

My writers group – **Sarada LeBourgeois, Gwen Plauché, Jessica Rapalo and Julie Andre'**– for being my Monday morning support group. You all are the best!

Acknowledgments

Eric Cantrelle –for your exciting and creative talents that resulted in the cover of this book.

Bobbie Alexander - for being the "midwife" to my baby, this book. I appreciate your expertise, time and patience.

Derek Lewis – for taking the hodgepodge of my talks and written materials and helping me organize them into a master format.

Nathan Martin – for being the publisher who saw signs of talent in me and for believing in my project.

And to all my friends who were there to support me. To all of you, from the bottom of my heart: Thank You!

INTRODUCTION

Who am I to tell you to get off your attitude?

I'm a normal guy who has failed, been hurt, made mistakes, been rejected, and lost nearly everything. I'm a dropout who has been shot, foreclosed on, fired, diagnosed as clinically depressed, dumped, and failed in business.

While those are interesting examples, what's worth reading is how I chose to respond to life and how I haven't let those experiences define me. This book isn't only about my life. It's about inspiring you to achieve a winning attitude in your own life.

I'm not a doctor, a psychologist, or a psychiatrist. I haven't done extensive research into human behavior. I'm not a counselor with years of experience. I am a person with 30-plus years of life experience.

For many years, I had the wrong attitude toward life and it seemed that life had the wrong attitude toward me. I felt the rules didn't apply. I expected trouble to find me, and it always did.

Despite my former approach to life, I've had several great opportunities. I've traveled as a promoter and speaker for Brian Tracy and other training organizations. I've served as the vice president of sales for two companies.

I've lived in some amazing places and was fortunate to meet several of the most incredible and successful people in this country. One thing I noticed about all of them was their positive attitude. They were happy, fulfilled, friendly, and enjoyed life. I learned that it wasn't because they had reached success. It was because they had a confident belief, not only in themselves, but also in life.

Being around them inspired me to search for a positive outlook for myself. The more optimistic I became, the more great things seemed to happen to me and the better my life became. The more I applied this positive attitude to specific areas of my life, the better I did in each area.

This took time, effort, and patience. The payoff was huge!

In this book, I'll discuss how to "get off your attitude" in these key areas. I'll challenge you to think about your beliefs and attitudes and help you examine how they affect your life. These key areas are:

- Your relationships
- Your dreams

Introduction

- Your time
- Your past
- Your present
- Your faith
- Your health
- Your finances
- Your gratefulness
- Your giving back

Chapter one lays the foundation for all of it and focuses on the importance of choosing the right attitude as a basic habit in life. The final chapter is about putting all of these attitudes into play in your life and making it happen!

I'll take you through the full spectrum of my experiences, from falling into the traps of life to crawling out, dusting myself off, and continuing my journey. I'll tell you about the wrong attitudes I had and how they led to wrong choices, and how having the right attitudes led to great decisions.

You'll learn about the people I love and the friendships I've enjoyed. You'll see other people who have inspired me and books I've read that helped me to become a better person.

I'll share:

- Principles for you to live by, "GOYA-isms;"
- Warm-up exercises, "GOYA-cises," to help you start applying these ideas in your day-to-day living;
- Real-life stories to illustrate each point;
- Quotes from others that you may find to be inspirational.

In other words, this is a book about life…with all its unsuspected pitfalls and amazing opportunities.

Having had my own epiphany, I now have a passion: to do all I can to help others achieve the life they've imagined by getting off their attitude.

"Get off your attitude" means:

- To think positive and take action;
- To talk, believe, act, and think in a positive manner;
- To create a positive mindset during a negative situation or environment;
- To help someone to create a positive mindset to overcome fear, adversity, oppression, or challenges that person may face in life.

Today I'm passionately pursuing my purpose in life: motivating other people through coaching, seminars, and books. I'm doing what I love…while hoping to help you achieve an even better life today than you had yesterday.

Do you feel stuck? Is life not treating you the way you want it to? It's not anyone or anything else. It's just you! Your attitude is the number one thing holding you back right now. The most life-changing thing I can tell you is the choice is yours—you have the power to change your life simply by changing your attitude. So—

Get off your attitude!

Chapter 1

Choose to Be Positive

Whether you think you can or think you can't,
you're right. —Henry Ford

ONE MORNING I WOKE UP at 4 A.M., heart pounding, skin sweating, and mind racing. In the span of a few years, I managed to lose just about everything—my company, my career, my home, my pride, and my self-confidence. I found myself right back where I had started my adult life—in my college town of Baton Rouge, renting a room from a friend, and scratching out a living in an entry-level sales job.

It happened quickly. I hadn't had time to process everything; but the anxiety, shame, and sense of failure were slowly getting to me. I rarely slept, and when I did, I tossed and turned, and woke up in a near panic. I was broke, financially and mentally. I felt as if I had fallen down a long, dark hole and everything was caving in on me. There were moments when I literally found it hard to breathe.

I kept asking myself where I had gone wrong. Had I been stupid and reckless? Did I choose the wrong job? What could I have done differently? I kept replaying my entire life in my head—all the choices I made or didn't make, the forks in the road I didn't take, and all the ways I could have prevented this disaster.

Have you ever had words pop into your head and you can't remember where you heard them? Maybe it was a bit of a song or a magazine you read some time ago? Several months before, I had been brainstorming and randomly wrote down four words. That morning around 4 A.M., those four words suddenly came back to me.

Get off your attitude.

I wasn't sure why I had remembered them at four in the morning, but I couldn't get them out of my head. I would go back to thinking about my bad luck and bad choices, but I couldn't shake that phrase. It just rolled around and around in my head—*get off your attitude.*

It kept repeating until I decided to say it out loud. I said, *"Hey, Ryan—get off your attitude!"*

Hearing those words out loud did something to me. I've always been a go-getter, but in the past few months I felt totally helpless as I watched my life slip through my hands. I felt that somehow everything was unfair and I didn't deserve all that had happened to me. But hearing those words made me realize I had been sitting around with a victim's mentality, waiting for life to get better. I realized I couldn't change what had happened. All I could change was my attitude about it.

I could choose how I would let the situation affect me and decide what I was going to do about it. Was I going to sit around whining for the rest of my life, or was I going to get off my attitude and do something about it!?

That night, I decided "get off your attitude" was my new mantra. I was not going to let my past determine my future. At that moment, I realized it was up to me to take responsibility for my life and shape my future—starting with my attitude.

The Importance of Attitude

Why is attitude so important? *Because it determines every-thing else in your life!*

Attitude isn't just about whether or not you're having a good or bad day. Attitude is more than that. It affects relationships. It affects careers. It affects your entire future.

I've met people who went through something similar to what I did. They were flying high, had a great business, and then lost it all. Years later, they're still talking about their problems and misfortunes. For some of them, their spouse left them and they were forced to sell the family business. With others, their business partner was cheating them. Some had their major customer go out of business.

These people are talented, experienced, and smart. If they would start another business, the odds of success this time could be quite good. Unfortunately, they're still reliving the events that led up to their failure. Their negative attitude won't let them get on with their life.

I know how they feel. I know what failure feels like. I lost my business. It hurts. What's the difference between those negative thinking people and me? It's our attitudes. I'm not any better than they are or any smarter than they are. I am different from them in one way: I chose to see my past and my future differently.

I GOT OFF MY ATTITUDE!

In *The Winning Attitude*, John Maxwell summed up the idea of attitude. Let me share it with you:

Attitude...
It is the "advance man" of our true selves.
Its roots are inward but its fruit is outward.
It is our best friend or our worst enemy.
It is more honest and more consistent than our words.
It is an outward look based on past experiences.
It is a thing which draws people to us or repels them.
It is never content until it is expressed.
It is the librarian of our past.
It is the speaker of our present.
It is the prophet of our future.

Can you see how important your attitude is? Changing your attitude can literally change your life. It did mine. And here's the great thing about attitude: *It's your choice.*

Want a Great Life?

Your attitude is a habit. Most people I meet have a bad habit of believing they can't do anything; of talking down to themselves, and of living a life of quiet defeat. They think, talk, and act as if it's impossible for them to succeed.

If this is you—stop it!

When I'm guilty of that, I remind myself of this truth:

Watch your thoughts, for they become words.
Watch your words, for they become actions.
Watch your actions, for they become habits.
Watch your habits, for they become character.
Watch your character, for it becomes your destiny.

—Unknown

Do you see it!? If you want to live a fulfilling life—one filled with an abundance of health, wealth, and happiness—it starts with how you think, talk, and act!

Living the life of your dreams starts with getting into a habit of being positive in how you think, talk, and act. That's it! The flip side of the coin is if you have a habit of thinking, talking, and acting negatively, you are living a life far below what you can achieve.

Two of my favorite books are *The Power of Positive Thinking* by Norman Vincent Peale and *Success through a Positive Mental Attitude* by Napoleon Hill and W. Clement Stone. These books underscore the basic idea that success and fulfillment in life begins with your thoughts.

GOYA-ism:

If you control your thoughts, and control your choices, you'll create a brighter future.

You Have a Choice

I hear some people say, "I can't help it. Somebody tells me something and I just react," or, "I can't help how I feel."

Children *react* to life; adults *respond* to it. Sure, when something happens, you instantly feel an emotion, whether it's grief, or anger, or anxiety. But immature people fail to realize they don't have to act immediately on that emotion. They can choose how to respond. When I'm tempted to just lash out at something, I remember something I once heard:

Life is 10% what happens to you and 90% how you respond to it. —Charles Swindoll

Some people believe they don't have a choice and that their fate is out of their hands—that God, life, the universe, or whoever, decides what will happen to them.

They have this passive approach to life that whatever happens, happens.

Yes, those things play into the big picture, but you have a choice of what you do about it. God gave me the phrase "get off your attitude." I could have dropped it or ignored it. I could have stayed negative with a victim's mentality. But I decided to do something.

You can do the same thing! You have the power to change your life. Believe this:

If there is anything you want to change in your world, change your attitude toward it.

That's my version of The Law of Attitude!

Life isn't about what happens to you—it's what you do about it. Honestly, you can't change much of what happens in life, but you can change how you look at it. That, in turn, changes everything.

In promoting Brian Tracy and other speaking and training organizations, I've had the privilege of living all over the United States and meeting some of the best and most successful people in the country. They all had different careers. They all came from different backgrounds. They all achieved different measures of wealth and success. But do you know the one thing they all had in common?

A positive attitude!

These people wake up in the morning *expecting* to succeed that day. If you could go back in time, you would find they all had a positive attitude *before* they started experiencing success.

What is success? This is how I define it:

> *Success is being able to do what you love*
> *and get paid for it.*

The inspiring people I have met loved what they were doing—and they got paid very well for doing it. These people weren't lucky. They simply approached life from a different angle and with a different set of expectations.

I hear people say, "Why doesn't anything good ever happen to me? Why do some people have all the luck?" Here's what being lucky means to me: being able to see life optimistically and realize opportunities are all around you. If you're going around with a negative attitude, you'll be blind to those opportunities. Positive people and "lucky opportunities" will pass you by because of your pessimism. As long as you keep that outlook, so-called luck will never find you.

Want to change your luck? Change your attitude!

Take the Negative Out, Plug the Positive In

Being positive is a habit. It takes time to realize all the negative thoughts, words, and actions you use in daily life. You must learn to recognize when you're being negative.

When you see it, you need to rid yourself of negativity and focus on something positive instead. I learned this life lesson in my Maw-maw's garden.

When I was about seven years old, I was helping my grandmother weed her tomato garden. Like any kid, I was tired of doing the same thing over and over again. Finally, I asked why we had to pull weeds all the time. She said if we didn't, the weeds would grow and eventually choke our tomatoes.

I said, "But Maw-maw, we weed all the time!"

She said, "Ryan, that's how it is—weeds are always going to grow, but if we keep pulling them, they won't damage and overrun our tomatoes, instead the tomatoes will grow to be fresh and ripe."

I don't know if my grandmother realized she was teaching me about life, but I believe she did. We have to constantly "weed" out negative thoughts, words, and actions or they'll continue to grow. Sometimes they're our own thoughts and sometimes we get them from somewhere else. But keeping our mind free and clear of negativity allows positive thoughts and ideas to grow.

One of the most influential books in my life was *Think and Grow Rich* by Napoleon Hill. He wrote about the Law of Attraction:

> *Our minds become magnetized with the dominating thoughts we hold...and these magnets attract to us the*

forces, the people, the circumstances of life which harmonize with the nature of our dominating thoughts. —
Napoleon Hill

We live in a society where we're bombarded with negativity all day long. We read about it in the newspapers and in our email; we listen to it on the radio; we watch it on television; and we hear it in many people around us. No one wakes up to a negativity-free world.

But those great people you meet in your life—the people who inspire you and make you want to be a better person like my grandmother, your Little League coach, or your favorite teacher—are those who constantly weed out bad influences and leave the good ones to grow. They control their life's harvest by planting good ideas, words, and actions. They plant positive seeds of abundance and harvest the benefits of it.

Remember, you are in control of your life and your future. It's your choice in how you face life's situations. Make the choice that a positive response is the only way to handle them. If you'll inject faith, hope, and love into your everyday living, you will see life open up. It will become something more meaningful and grand.

Start with your thoughts. Brian Tracy says:

You become what you think about most of the time.

Your reality—the life you'll live—begins in your mind. Here's an interesting fact—your mind can only hold one thought at a time. If it can only hold one, you might as well choose a positive one.

I tell people it's just like listening to a radio with only two stations—one's negative and one's positive. If you don't like what you're hearing on WNEG, switch to the positive station—WPOS. You can change your life just as easily as you changed the station!

WNEG	WPOS
No, that's impossible.	I know it's possible.
This is a huge problem.	It's a huge opportunity.
I wish I could have that.	How can I achieve that?
I can't afford it.	How can I afford it?
I don't have what it takes.	I do have what it takes.

Stop dwelling on the bad and start focusing on the good. I mean, it's not rocket science. How hard is it to see that if you're always pessimistic, you'll be a miserable person who never achieves their dreams? Or, if you always see the good in every situation, you'll achieve great things in life?

I read about a study which concluded the average person thinks about 60,000 thoughts a day. A separate study concluded eight out of every ten thoughts of the average person are generally negative. Eighty percent! Combined, these two studies say you have about 48,000 negative thoughts a day. No wonder so many people have a bad attitude!

With all that fear, doubt, and anger flowing through your mind daily, it's easy to see why you have a hard time believing this positive attitude stuff. It's a miracle you can believe anything good. These studies highlight what I call NAB—"negative attitude blockage." If you have a heart blockage, it deprives your body of life-giving blood. If you don't take action immediately, it could be life-threatening.

NAB works the same way. Negativity blocks life-giving hope and belief to your mind and spirit. If you don't take action, it could be fatal, and it could deprive you of the best things in life.

In my seminars, I break this concept into an easy-to-remember formula:

Positive Thoughts + Positive Feelings = Positive Actions

You will achieve the life you've imagined, beginning with your thoughts.

If you could go back in time and visit a successful person when they were unknown, I would bet they wouldn't be talking about how bad their life was, how much they hated their job, or how nobody would listen to their ideas. You would hear them talking about their dreams, the good fortune they would soon enjoy, and how great things were going to be. Early in their lives, they adopted the habit of being positive.

Choose to Be Positive

During one part of my career, I trained others how to set and achieve their goals. I was paid to talk about being positive. Yet during that time, I was making bad choices in my personal life. In retrospect, I see I had issues with self-confidence and self-image. I threw my own pity parties and played the victim. I encouraged other people to be positive about their lives, and yet I see now, I wasn't positive about mine.

Sometimes a person's true self is hard to see. I acted as if I had a positive attitude, but I wasn't truly positive. I had a negative attitude about myself and my life. That is why having the right attitude isn't something superficial. It needs to become the very core of who and what you are.

When you start thinking positive, you start talking positive, and then acting positive. Words are perhaps the most powerful tools you possess. The idea of how powerful they are goes as far back as biblical times. The book of Proverbs says:

Death and life are in the power of the tongue.

When I grasped this idea, I began to affirm my belief in myself and my dreams every day. When I hear those howling winds of doubt, I turn up the volume on WPOS. I realize how powerful words are. I use them to my advantage and to enrich the lives of those around me. Do you?

Live a Great Life Everyday

My own acronym of "attitude" is:

Always
Take
The
Initiative
To
Uncover
Daily
Enthusiasm

It means you're looking for the good in every situation and in every person, every day, all the time. Having a positive attitude is not simply a hope or wishful thinking. I know firsthand life isn't always great. But the fact remains, you can look at it in an optimistic way.

I once attended a seminar where the presenter asked, "When you wake up in the morning, do you say, 'Good morning, God!' or 'Good God, it's morning.'" What's your attitude? How do you start your day?

What do you do on a daily basis? Are you acting on your positive thoughts and words? If you believe you can find a better job, are you optimistically searching—and expecting to find something better? If you say your relationship with your significant other is going to be better, are you actively engaging in better behavior?

People ask me what are some of my daily habits. I tell them I eat three square meals a day. For breakfast, I read a success story on the internet. For lunch, I listen to a motivational speaker. For dinner, I watch an inspiring biography. By constantly feeding myself great mental and emotional food, I find it's pretty easy to stay in great shape!

I'm not someone who's lived a perfect life. I've made some bad—sometimes really bad—decisions. By choosing to have a positive outlook, I've turned my life into something very positive.

My choice to be positive helped me get my life back on track. If you will infuse your life with positive energy, incredible things will happen. It's not some sort of magical formula. It's just the way life works.

Take this idea to heart—everything in life begins with your attitude, and that is the one thing you completely control. This key idea—how you choose to respond to circumstances—determines how those circumstances affect your entire life. Get into the habit of thinking, talking, and acting positive about everything.

Choose to be positive. Choose your destiny.

GOYA-cise:

Start noticing how you think, talk, and act. When you think or say something negative, find a way to switch it to something positive. Decide to find the good in

every person and situation. Spend a little time listening to, watching, or reading inspiring stories and
people. Throughout the day, use positive affirmation,
such as: "I am responsible for my life. I will choose to
respond with a positive attitude."

Now that you know the secret to achieving a better
life, I want to encourage you to go after your dreams. But
before you can reach for them, you have to surround yourself with positive people who are going to help you soar.

Chapter 2

Soar With the Eagles

Eagles come in all shapes and sizes, but you
will recognize them chiefly by their attitudes.
—Charles Prestwich Scott

Right now, a guy who's like a brother to me, may be looking at prison time. He's not a bad person. He hasn't hurt anybody or scammed anyone. He just fell in with the wrong group of business associates who turned out to be frauds. By the time he realized who he was working with, it was too late—his name was already in the newspapers. I look at his situation—at how it's affecting his life and his family—and constantly remind myself of the importance of surrounding myself with the right people.

I must emphasize how important your relationships are to your well-being. High performance expert Dr. Denis Waitley said:

*Take a good look at your friends
and you will see your future.*

You will become like the people you surround yourself with. It's a fact. Countless studies and common sense show that you are heavily influenced by the people with whom you spend the most time. The great thing is you can choose these people. This is very important. It's a life-changing choice. You've got to surround yourself with eagles!

What Are Eagles?

Think about someone who had a profound influence on your life. Maybe it was your coach in high school or a professor in college. It could have been a member of your family. It could have been a pastor or one of your parents' friends. Whoever it was, they made a strong impact on your life and you're better for having known them.

Those are eagles—great people who want to see you succeed in life. They've inspired you to be a better person. They've taken you under their wings and helped guide you toward the right choices in life. They've been your mentors and your friends. They helped you become who you are today.

Did you know that when it rains, the eagle is the only bird that flies above the clouds to avoid the rain? In life, eagles do the same—they fly above the negativity.

Soar With the Eagles

One of my eagles was my grandmother—"Maw-maw." She was more than just a grandparent—she was one of my very best friends. She spent what we now call "quality time" with me and taught me about life. She was kind, compassionate, and wise. I learned about love and respect, faith in God and myself, and how to be a better person. She was always nurturing me and helping me enjoy my childhood. In her garden, around her table, and on trips into and from New Orleans, she shared her life with me.

Maw-maw didn't expect me to be perfect—she just wanted me to do my best. In turn, I never wanted to let her down. I wanted her to be proud of me—to tell me I had done well. To this day, I measure much of my life by how much Maw-maw would approve and whether she would think I had done my best. The positive choices I've made in my life are, to a large degree, because of her influence.

Most of my eagles today are still my family and friends. My parents, sister, and my brothers are wonderful people. I make sure I nurture my relationships. Some of my friendships stretch back to elementary school. I want to be around people who love me, support me, and influence me to be a better person.

What do my eagles look like?

- Energetic
- Encouraging
- Loving/caring
- Compassionate

- Empathetic
- Giving
- Humorous

My eagles hold me accountable and are honest with me about myself. They avoid prejudice, jealously, and drama.

You see, eagles don't just care about you. They care about you to the point that they'll call you out when you deserve it. They love you enough that they'll challenge you to be a better person.

Here's a challenge for you: Write down the characteristics of the people who have had a great influence on your life. What were they like? What did they put into your life?

What Are Owls?

A stranger in a coffee shop once told me:

You can't soar with the eagles during the day
if you're bumming around with the owls at night.

Not everyone in your life can be an inspiring mentor. Be careful about bumming around with the owls. To some degree, these people are the opposite of eagles. Maybe they're not trying to tear you down, but their influence is holding you back. Most of the owls I know don't have bad intentions, but their words, their spirit, and their attitude drag me down. I'll give you an example.

I have a friend who's a good guy, but every time we would get together for coffee, he would start talking about how terrible his job was; how much he hated his boss; how messed up the company was; and how unhappy he was in life. I tried to be an eagle and encourage him to cheer up and find another position, but I never seemed to get through to him. Instead of helping him, I would leave depressed! Eventually, I had to distance myself from him because his attitude was affecting me.

Please don't think I'm saying you need to approach relationships with a "what's-in-it-for-me" mentality. Soaring with the eagles is about engaging in *positive* relationships. That means both people have to be investing in it. It can't be one-sided.

Dr. Steve Ornelas wrote a book entitled *Energy Vampires*. Just like my friend, these are people who suck the life right out of you—and they're often unaware they're doing it! Don't let people steal your energy. Realize when your life is being sucked out of you and get away from them.

Here's another example of one of these energy vampires—a true owl if I've ever heard of one. I knew an entrepreneur who finally opened his own small business. He worked day and night on the place. It was exhausting, but he was still excited.

About a week before his grand opening, an old high school friend stopped by to see him. His friend walked around and didn't say much. Right before the friend left, he sarcastically told the entrepreneur, "I guess you think you've made it, huh?" He was so jealous and insecure that he couldn't even be happy for the entrepreneur's hard work and years of sacrifice. He tried to suck the life and excitement right out of him.

Eagles want you to soar with them in the bright daylight; owls want you hang around with them in the gloomy darkness. Be happy for people who have achieved success or something positive in their life. Don't be envious. Celebrate their success and become an eagle yourself.

Go back to the list you made of eagles' characteristics. Next to each characteristic, list its opposite. You'll quickly have a list of the traits of people you want to hang around, and another one of the people you need to avoid.

Who Are Your Eagles and Owls?

As you made those two lists, I'm sure you had specific people in mind. You already know who your eagles and owls are. Which ones are you surrounding yourself with? Look at who you spend your time with, because that's who you'll become. If you're making the choice to get off your attitude, to change your life, and to become a more successful person, you need to hang around more eagles.

Surround yourself with only people who are going to lift you higher. —Oprah Winfrey

One of the hardest things you'll ever do is sever—or at least diminish—your relationship with someone who is a bad influence. Maybe a family member or a friend is an owl and always discourages you from doing any better than you are now. I'm not saying you have to stop having that relationship altogether, but you're not going to be much better than you are now unless you limit how much they influence you.

There's a poem by an unknown author that constantly reminds me of the importance of relationships. It begins like this:

People come into your life for a reason,
a season, or a lifetime.

Recognize some of the relationships you've had only last for a specific time or perhaps for a single purpose. Learn to let life flow. Don't force it. Make a choice to let go of your owls and surround yourself with people who are going to lift you higher.

How do you find eagles? My parents used to say, "Birds of a feather flock together." That's true of eagles. They're everywhere. They tend to stick with their own kind instead of bumming around with the owls. If you want to find eagles, start acting like one. You'll be attracted to like-minded people and they'll be attracted to you. You must put out positive energy so others can identify you as an eagle.

Go back to your list of eagles' characteristics. Start embodying those traits. Be that uplifting, encouraging person other people want to be around. Take other people under your own wing.

Fly High

When I lived in Dallas, a few friends and I created a mastermind group that I now call an "eagles' nest." Once a month, we'd get together with about twenty or so like-minded people. It wasn't a formal group and we didn't concentrate on networking. Our focus was reaching out to each other, inspiring one another, and sharing information which could help motivate everyone professionally.

I've maintained some of those relationships, especially the one with my buddy and mentor, Jim Monk. When I came up with "get off your attitude" his response was: "You need to run with that!" He encouraged me and held me accountable at the same time. That's what eagles do. They encourage you and then they hold you accountable!

GOYA-ism:

Find people that stimulate you, educate you, and challenge you!

Surrounding myself with confident, helpful people and engaging in positive relationships keeps me motivated and helps me become a better person. Charlie "Tremendous" Jones said:

You will be the same person in five years as you are today except for the people you meet and the books you read.

Who do you want to be in five years? If you want to be a different person, you need to find mentors and role models with whom you can start a friendship. If they're true eagles, they'll be glad to reach back and help you. Behind every eagle is at least one other eagle who helped them get where they are. Your mentor knows they can't ever repay that person. Instead of paying it back, pay it forward.

Be open-minded. Eagles come in all shapes, forms, and sizes. They can also be authors, speakers, athletes, etc. They don't necessarily have to have a close in-person relationship with you.

Remember, some may come into your life for a reason, some for a season, and some for a lifetime. The important thing is to cultivate a great relationship and receive what they have to give.

Act like an eagle, surround yourself with eagles, and soon you will be an eagle!

GOYA-cise:

List the traits of an eagle and the traits of an owl. Think about each of the people in your life right now.

Do you share similar characteristics with them? With the eagles? With the owls? Identify your eagles and start spending more time being influenced by them. Start your own eagles' nest—a group of like-minded individuals who come together for the express purpose of helping each other toward a common goal.

Eagles not only challenge you to be a better person, but also, like Jim, they encourage you to go after your dreams. Engage in positive relationships and find people who will support you as you discover your calling in life and then, pursue it passionately.

Chapter 3

Dream Out Loud

*Too many of us are not living our dreams
because we are living our fears.* —Les Brown

MY MOTHER STARTED an antique store with one piece of furniture and a dream. Through hard work, determination, and a belief in herself, she turned it into one of the largest antique stores in the area. It wasn't something that happened overnight. It took time.

It also took the whole family. My dad would come home from his full-time job at the utility company and spend nights and weekends polishing, repairing, and refinishing furniture. All six of us—my parents, my two brothers, my sister, and I—put a lot of time into the family business. I'm glad I was able to be part of that and watch my mother's dream come true. My father believed in her every step of the way. Together, we built something we could take pride in.

Growing up with entrepreneurs for parents, I knew I wanted to have my own business one day. In 2007, I had my chance. A business associate approached me and offered me the opportunity to become a partner in his new insurance company and to serve as the vice president of sales. I immediately accepted. Over the next two years, we built a great company and enjoyed success. I was watching my dream of being a business owner unfold right before my eyes.

The economic recession completely blindsided our industry. Our company was affected along with hundreds of others in the financial sector. Everything quickly fell apart. We were among the first victims of the brewing economic recession.

For a while, I didn't know what to do. I felt that life had handed me my dreams and just when I had wrapped my hands around them, life snatched them away. I was hurt, angry, and confused. That's why I was waking up at four in the morning panicked and anxious. I had no idea what had happened or what to do next.

Looking back, I see my real problem was that I had lost sight of my lifelong dreams. I had set them on a shelf. You see, I didn't only dream to have my own business—I also wanted to be a motivational speaker and author. While I was a business partner, those dreams seemed to be within reach. But after the business collapsed, I felt foolish and ashamed for ever thinking about them.

There I was, living out of a friend's spare room while working an entry-level sales job. I couldn't see any way to go from there to being a motivational speaker, author, and entrepreneur. So I shelved the dreams and trudged on with a miserable, bleak life.

The morning when I started telling myself to get off my attitude, I decided to take my dreams down from that shelf and dust them off. I realized that I had had some setbacks, but I knew I wasn't out of the game for good!

I knew what I wanted to do. I was going to start a company to inspire people the same way I was inspired—with the message to *get off your attitude*!

As soon as I had the thought, I immediately started to doubt it. Who was I to tell people to get off their attitude? I didn't know anything about writing a book. I didn't have the money to start another business. But I realized I was thinking about my dream with a negative attitude. I switched channels to WPOS and started envisioning myself helping people through my seminars and books. I envisioned living my dream of having my own business again. I saw myself where I am today.

I've been fortunate to speak to a variety of groups and organizations, provide training, and even write the book you're holding. Was it hard work? Did it take blind faith? Did I sometimes have to jump without seeing where I would land? Yes, and it has been worth all the cost, the effort, and the sacrifice.

Stop Saying "I Can't!"

You can! Success requires action! The only reason I'm passionately pursuing my purpose is that I changed my attitude toward it. I decided to believe I could go after my dreams. That's the only thing keeping you from reaching your dreams—your self-limiting beliefs.

Stop telling yourself it will never work, or it's foolish, or it's impractical. Stop making excuses about why you don't have enough time or why you need to wait until later. My mother had four children and a husband and still found time to see her dreams come true.

We weren't neglected because my mother was focused on her work. I was fortunate to be a part of that! When you go after your dreams, include others in it. It will make the journey much more worthwhile. I shared my dreams and my goals with my family, friends, and girlfriend. They encouraged me and helped me reach those dreams. Sharing your dreams with others helps you to commit to them.

If you're not going after your dreams now, do you know why? It's not because of money, timing, family, or anything else. It's because you're afraid—afraid of failure, ridicule, loss, and everything else. It's called "fear."

In my seminars, I use this acronym many speakers use:

False
Evidence
Appearing
Real

That's the one I tell people the most, but my favorite acronym is:

Forget
Everything
And
Run

That's how fear affects you! You have a gut reaction and want to stay away from that feeling. We need to be more like kids. They have no fear, they're relentless, and they don't take "no" for an answer. When they want something, they don't stop until they get it. Imitate them. It works!

Listen to me: Going after your dreams is tough. You'll have to get out of your comfort zone. But if you never leave the comfortable little place you've made for yourself, you'll never grow. Here is what I tell people:

GOYA-ism:

You must do something you're not used to doing, to get something you're not used to getting.

That's why only a few people succeed. They're the few who left the safe harbor and sailed into uncharted waters.

It's okay if you don't think of yourself as an adventurous risk-taker. You don't need to be some kind of star athlete or made of "the right stuff" to go after your dreams. Anyone can.

Dreams come in all sizes. Maybe you've always wanted to be a teacher, own your own business, or be a respected athlete. You might want to play the piano or write poetry. Whatever it is, you can do it!

I was tempted to wait until I had recovered from my failures and disappointments to begin again. But I was too excited to wait! I didn't allow my doubts to stop me. Speaking and helping others has been my passion. I can't imagine going back to the life I was living—one where I saw only problems and never saw the possibilities.

Is your disbelief holding you back? Stop saying: "I can't."

Believe!

Tell yourself you can!

Whatever the mind of man can conceive and believe, it can achieve. —Napoleon Hill

Any time you think or say something negative about your dreams, you must stop yourself. Realize you're setting yourself up for failure. Get out of the habit of failing before you start.

GOYA-ism:

It's okay to be afraid.
It's not okay to stop or give up.

Don't Hide From Your Dreams

What are your dreams? Don't tell me you don't have any. You do. Maybe you're too ashamed or afraid to say them out loud—or to even think about them—but you have them. I believe every one of us has a unique purpose to fill—a calling. Do you ever hear your dream? Do you ever feel it tug on your heart or whisper in your ear? It's that something that lifts your heart and gets you excited by just thinking about it.

I remember when I left the speaking business for a while to go into a corporate setting. Every time I would go to a speaking event or a seminar, my pulse would race because I would imagine myself as the one on stage. I would tell whomever I was with, "I would love to be doing that!" When you start to drift away from your dream, it will call out to you and you will attract and discover the means to make it happen.

You may not even realize you've stumbled upon your dream. Perhaps you haven't discovered your passion yet,

GET OFF YOUR ATTITUDE

but I promise it exists for you. Even if you don't know it, your subconscious is finding the people, ideas, and resources to enable you to achieve it.

Life leaves you clues on what you're supposed to be doing. After I came up with "get off your attitude," I immediately went to the internet. I was sure the domain name was taken. I mean, it was 2009—*everything* had been taken. But to my surprise, getoffyourattitude.com was available. So I claimed it. My friends later said, "How did you manage *that*!?" It just goes to show you—anything's possible.

Here was a real affirmation that I was on the right track. About four months after that revelation, I came home and decided to browse through my library. I came across my grandmother's Bible which my mother had passed on to me a few years earlier. It was one of those old Bibles with a black vinyl cover and a zipper all the way around it. On a whim, I decided to leaf through it. As soon as I unzipped it, the first thing I saw was a bookmark which read:

Attitude

One part at a time, one day at a time, we can accomplish any goal we set for ourselves. Today, I will do one small task that will contribute toward the achievement of a life goal.

That was my sign. I knew I was doing what I was supposed to be doing—helping people to get off their attitude and reach for their dreams!

What are your dreams? *Write them down!* It's not enough to just think about them—you need to write them down, carry them with you, and tape them to the bathroom mirror. This will remind you every day what they are. Then, do at least one small task each day that will contribute toward the achievement of a life goal.

If you know your dreams, write down all the reasons why you know it's what you're supposed to do. If you haven't discovered your dreams yet, start noticing the things you're attracted to, what excites you, what keeps crossing your path, and what keeps seeping into your thoughts.

See Your Dreams

As soon as you find or rediscover your dreams, you need to "dream out loud." By that I mean make your dream as real as possible. Think about them, talk about them, daydream about them. Do whatever it takes to keep them as alive and as real as possible. Act on them.

I used to imagine myself in front of an audience, speaking and signing books. By the time I had my first opportunity to speak, I had already performed in front of millions of imaginary people and signed thousands of imaginary books. You need to do the same thing and see yourself living out your dreams.

One day at work, a co-worker helped me understand the importance of this. After sharing my dream of being a motivational speaker with him, he went to his office and shut the door. He copied the biography and picture of a well-known motivational speaker from a website, but replaced the picture and the name with mine. A few minutes later, he came out and presented me with his gift. "Ryan, you need to keep your vision in front of you. You need to see yourself as that great motivational speaker." Talk about encouraging!

> *If one advances confidently in the direction of his dreams, and endeavors to live the life which he has imagined, he will meet with success unexpected in common hours.* — Henry David Thoreau

I love that quote! "The life which he has imagined"— what an awesome phrase! Thoreau had it right. When you have a confident attitude toward your dreams, and start taking bold strides to reach them, you'll meet with unexpected success. Don't settle for less than you deserve— live the life you've imagined!

Albert Einstein had a similar inspirational phrase:

> *Your imagination is your preview of life's coming attractions.*

GOYA-ism:

A visionary is a person who has one foot in the present and one in the future at the same time.

In other words, they can be realistic about their current circumstances while still imagining what their destiny could be.

You can be a visionary, too. Do what my co-worker did for me—make a "vision poster" with all the images, words, and whatever else helps you to "preview life's coming attractions."

Stay Away From "Dream-busters"

Who doesn't like the movie *Rocky*? What an inspiring story! After its debut, it quickly became an American classic, going on to win three Academy Awards. Did you know there were critics who said no one would watch it— that it would be a total flop? The story itself shows that belief and persistence will win out against skill alone and defeat the odds every time.

Let me be the first to warn you if no one else has: When you find your dreams, you will also find people who will try to keep you from them. They won't understand and they won't support you. Sometimes, these are well-intentioned people—people who love you, like your family or your friends. They'll say it's impossible, or you don't have the brains, or it's never been done, or anything else to discourage you from taking the risk.

Sometimes they may make fun of you and make you feel like you've come up with the dumbest idea in the world.

They are what I call "dream-busters." I stay as far away from these people as I can. I don't talk about my dreams around dream-busters because I can guess what they'll say. My dreams are my children and I certainly wouldn't let others talk negatively about my children. I protect and nurture my dreams and make sure I surround them with the best influences.

When dream-busters talk, what you really hear are their own fears and insecurities. When I first thought about getting into the speaking business, I shared that with a friend of mine. He said, "Ryan, do you know how many motivational speakers are out there? You don't have a chance!"

Wow, some friend, huh? I thought about what he said and realized he was a dream-buster, and I moved on. I knew I had a purpose to help and inspire other people. I wasn't going to let his insecurities and fears keep me from achieving the life I wanted.

You'll encounter naysayers like my friend. Others will mock you. People may say you're crazy. You'll even doubt yourself. Refuse to give in to the negativity. During times like these, think, talk, and act as though your dreams will come true—and they will.

Dream-busters are owls to the extreme. Go back to your list of owls from "Soar with the Eagles" and make sure you're careful not to tell those owls about your dreams.

How Do You Go After Your Dreams?

You act!

My friend Ruben Gonzalez, a business consultant and four-time Olympian, says it this way:

If you're not willing to take action, do us all a favor and STOP TALKING ABOUT IT!

As Lao Tzu said, *The journey of a thousand miles begins with a single step.* The same is true for the journey toward your dreams—it simply comes down to putting one foot in front of the other.

1. *Goals*—break your ultimate dream down into smaller goals. These are the little successes you'll achieve along the way. When I was ready to go after my dream of writing a book, the first thing I did was decide on the main theme that would become the title. Then I gathered my material and my thoughts. Then I found someone to design the cover. Then I found an editor.

When you break your big dream into bite-size goals, you won't feel overwhelmed and you start making those bold strides toward the life you've imagined.

Think of setting and achieving goals as constructing the building blocks to your ultimate dreams.

2. *Sacrifice*—be ready to pay the price for your dream. (Whatever it is, it's worth it!) When I decided to become

a motivational speaker, I didn't have people knocking down my door to come speak to their group. I had to work two jobs, and even had to move in with my parents for a few months. Can you imagine moving back in with your parents in your thirties? It all comes down to this question: How bad do you want it?

I once had an experience which gave me a fresh perspective on this question.

At the time, the girl I dated was an LSU student. I was planning on taking her to a game in Tiger Stadium one weekend. The Friday before the game, her professor assigned a huge project which was due the following Monday. It meant she would have to miss the game.

If you know me, you will know I've always been a huge Louisiana State University football fan. I was so disappointed. Who would even think about missing an LSU game, much less assign a project at the last minute to make sure everyone missed it? I was convinced he had some kind of mean streak, and I told her what I thought. She said, "He told us we should be working on our dreams instead of watching someone else achieve theirs."

Those words have always stayed with me. Even today, I ask myself, "Do I want to sit on the sidelines of life or do I want to get in the game?"

GOYA-ism:

You have to give up to get up.

3. *Patience*—you won't achieve your dreams overnight. As you travel on the path toward them, you'll probably get frustrated. Just writing this book has been a lesson in patience for me. I thought authors simply sat down and wrote a book. This has taken several attempts. It takes research, formulating ideas, and much, much more.

But patience and perseverance pay off—in dividends. Some of your dreams may happen in just a few days. Some may take years. But remember—however long it takes, it's worth it.

4. *Flexibility*—sometimes there's a detour—potholes you must maneuver around. You have to stay flexible. Change is the one constant in life, so you have to be constantly ready to change. I thought I would have been a full-time speaker and had my book written much sooner. But, even though things didn't work out exactly as I planned, I stayed on course!

The same will be true for you. Don't get bent out of shape because things look different than you expected. Roll with the punches and confidently keep advancing toward your dreams.

41

5. *Belief*—you must believe in your dreams. This is the key ingredient in reaching them. Belief chases away the fear and doubt, quiets the naysayers, and gives you the confidence to go after your dreams—no matter what. There is risk in doing anything new. But don't let the danger of those risks keep you from acting!

Never Give Up!

I'm grateful my parents taught me to never give up. I think of them each time I hear the Winston Churchill quote:

Never, never, never give up!

Watching my parents grow the business even when it was tough was inspiring. Their example instilled that same can-do attitude in me.

Remember Judy Garland singing "Somewhere Over the Rainbow"? I love the last line: "Where the dreams that you dare to dream really do come true." Dare to dream—and then never give up. Surround yourself with people and stories that inspire you to keep chasing your dream.

Some people use their age as an excuse not to pursue their life's passion. I tell them the story of Colonel Sanders. Who would take a 65-year-old honorary colonel wearing a string tie seriously? Using his social security check for gas money, he traveled around asking people to buy his fried chicken franchise. Today, "The Colonel" is one of America's favorite icons. You can start your dream at any age!

I also draw inspiration from Thomas Edison, who was said to be "stupid" and "un-teachable." He was fired from every job he ever had and was a great disappointment to his parents. In spite of his failings, Edison went on to obtain 1,093 patents and is considered one of the greatest geniuses of our time.

When people give me the excuse they don't have what it takes, I ask them: What are the odds of a single mother on welfare writing a best-selling book? And yet J. K. Rowling's *Harry Potter* series made her one of the wealthiest women in the world.

Let me ask you this: Could you vote for someone who had lost eight elections, bankrupted two businesses, and suffered a nervous breakdown? Thank goodness many did. The world would be a very different place if Abraham Lincoln hadn't been elected.

These people are the same as Joan of Arc, Sam Walton, Oprah Winfrey, Henry Ford, Richard Branson, Martin Luther King Jr., Mother Teresa, and John D. Rockefeller. They all came from modest, even poor, backgrounds. They weren't born to great wealth and many of them had personal handicaps. Yet they achieved success and their place in history not because of luck or chance, but because of their positive attitude toward their purpose in life.

GOYA-cise:

Write your dreams and goals on a piece of paper and read them two or three times a day. You'll be amazed how positive it makes you feel. Notice how you think, talk, and act about them. Is it self-limiting or self-liberating? Break down your dreams into individual goals. They're the small steps you take in the long journey. Finally, every day, do one small task that will contribute toward the achievement of your life's dreams.

Recently I had the opportunity to watch a biography about one of my favorite people, Walt Disney. Did you know his father once told him he would never make a living as an artist and that he had once been fired for drawing on the job? Some people discouraged him from pursuing his dreams. He was laughed out of bankers' offices for wanting to build DisneyLand®. He even had a nervous breakdown.

But his passion for his dreams kept him going. There's a phrase he was known to use often and which probably helped him to manage his time and to live a productive life:

Get on with it.

That phrase has helped me to do the same when dealing with procrastination and time management.

Chapter 4

GET ON WITH IT

Lost time is never found again.
—Benjamin Franklin

F YOU HAVE NEVER HAD the chance to see a New Orleans cemetery, you missed something special. They're not morbid rows of headstones. They're beautiful cities of stone; the monuments and mausoleums are works of art. Weeping angels, cathedral-like monuments, granite statues, wrought-iron fences, marble tombs worthy of royalty—they are breathtaking. It feels like walking through an old church.

There's a sense of a sacred peace as you walk by shrine after shrine memorializing life. Your life pauses as you feel a delicate tug on your heart and mind.

Whenever I find myself unfocused or unhappy, I take a walk in one of these cemeteries to remind myself that life is short and time is precious. That may sound strange. It's a great reminder that time is a gift I need to cherish and respect, and that I need to do something worthwhile NOW!

I'll stop in front of someone's grave and calculate how long they lived. I see their beginning and their end date. I wonder what they did with the time they had. Did they pursue their passion? Did they spend their life in love with someone? Did they enjoy their friends and family? Did they live life to the fullest?

Or did they waste their precious time and constantly procrastinate? Did they live in fear and regret? Did they live each day mulling over petty grievances and nursing old grudges? Did they play it safe and only do what they were expected to do? Did they take their time on earth for granted?

Wandering around in those cities of stone, I can almost hear the voices of generations past asking me what I'm doing with my life. Am I wasting it? Or am I living every minute to the fullest?

Think about it like this: If you knew you only had five more years to live, would it change your perspective on life? Would you suddenly value your time much more, and do more with it?

That's what these cemetery trips do for me—they reinforce the need to have the right attitude about time.

I'm not promised another thirty years on earth. I'm not even promised another thirty minutes. No one is. It's a great reminder that time is a gift.

How Do You Spend Your Time?

Time is like money—you spend it on your priorities.

While working in Dallas, I realized my nephews were growing up without me. I wanted to spend more time with them and the rest of my family. I moved back to Louisiana to spearhead expansion of my company into the state. It was one of the best personal decisions I've ever made.

I've been able to spend time on what's important to me. I've drawn closer to my wonderful parents and had the blessing of seeing my niece and nephews as they grow up. At the end of my life, I don't want to regret how I spent my time. I want to know I put my time where it was important.

Time is like money that you can deposit into something and get a return on your investment. By investing money, you have the opportunity to make more money. With time, you can't get more, but by investing it wisely you can enjoy the things money can't buy. If you invest time in people, you'll enjoy great relationships. If you invest time in your education, you'll be more valuable to everyone around you. If you invest your time in your faith, you'll have more peace and confidence.

Time is far more valuable than money. You can make more money—you can't make more time. Once a moment is gone, it's gone forever.

The important thing is to make sure you're as productive as you can be in every moment. I'm not talking about being an efficiency maniac. In *The 7 Habits of Highly Effective People*, Stephen Covey says it like this:

The key is not to prioritize what's on your schedule, but to schedule your priorities.

Just because you spend forty hours a week at your job and only twenty hours on the weekend with your family doesn't mean your job is more important than your family. You have to work to eat, right? You have responsibilities and obligations you have to fulfill. Your livelihood is highly important, but are you sacrificing time in other areas of your life for your career?

However, you have to be careful about letting the little things in life take priority over the big things. Having a clean house is important, but are you obsessing about it to the point you're spending less time with your children?

Are your dreams important to you? If they are, do you spend time pursuing them? Do you realize when you decide to watch pointless TV shows or play computer games that you could have been spending time pursuing your passion? The saying goes, "A fool and his money are soon parted." The same is true for time. If you don't spend your time wisely, you'll sit around and wonder where it all went.

Have you ever kept a time journal where you write down exactly how you spent every minute of every day over the course of a few days? Do it. I promise you'll be amazed how much time you spend on the mundane and how little you spend on important things.

How Much Is Time Worth?

It depends on who you are.

Successful people realize the value of time. They understand time is all you really have, and they make the most of it. As Stephen Covey says, they schedule their priorities. It's similar to a monthly financial budget. At the top of the budget are the necessities—food, utilities, rent/ mortgage, and the bills you absolutely have to pay. Toward the bottom of the list are the things you'd like to buy if there's enough money left over—treating yourself to a nice dinner or an expensive luxury.

You should prioritize your time the same way. At the top of the list are the things most important. For me, that's my faith and my family. After that come my career and my dreams. While I may spend more time on my career in a normal week than I do with my family, I budget time for my family first—then I budget time for my career. If at the end of the week I've spent all the time I budgeted and

I have some left over, then I'll treat myself to something, like a book, or a round of golf or a movie just for fun.

Are you a procrastinator? Okay, do you want to talk about this later?

I used to be one. I was sometimes late for meetings and projects, but I thought it was okay. Everybody is late sometimes, right?

It turns out not everyone. I had a valuable experience that really helped me gain a better perspective on time. I had scheduled a meeting with an important client. Although I tried to be on time, I was late. He didn't wait. Not only did it cost me the immediate sale but it cost me the whole relationship. It was a painful and expensive lesson, but one I learned well.

I'm sorry to see people who don't realize time's value. I love hanging out with others and having a good time, but I know some people who seem like they're constantly wasting time texting incessantly, complaining, or just going on and on about nothing.

We all need downtime—some space just to relax and unwind—but for the people I'm talking about, it's their part-time job! Their time isn't important, so what they do with it isn't important, either.

Be aware of time robbers. They could be these people, pointless activities, or simple distractions. Don't let these things steal your time. As Benjamin Franklin said, you'll never get that time back.

I want to pour my time into my life, my family, my faith, my career, and others. I look forward to enjoying every moment and every second of life. I think about what others have accomplished with time, and I imagine what I'll be able to do with mine. One of them is checking off all the items on my GOYA list.

Do you know what a "bucket list" is—all the things you want to do before you "kick the bucket"? I have my *"Get Off Your Attitude"* list. It's a list of everything I want to change my attitude toward. I never want to look back on my life and regret anything because I had the wrong attitude toward it.

What about you? Is time something you feel guilty about? Is time your friend or your enemy? Is it a tool to be used or something to battle?

Here's something to help you remember how valuable your time is: Write yourself a check for how much you'd like to earn per hour. Fifty, a hundred, a thousand dollars an hour—whatever you believe you can do. Tape it to your computer, television, or telephone—anywhere you know you waste time. When you're tempted to waste time, look at the check and then ask yourself if it's worth it.

Live in the Now

One of the most important attitudes you can adopt is to fully live in each moment. I'm not saying you have to be in the middle of an adventure every minute you're awake. I mean you need to live in the present.

For example, if you're having coffee with someone, be fully there. Don't be half-listening as you think about what happened yesterday or what you want to do tomorrow. Don't try to be half there and half somewhere else. Be there, in that moment, with them.

Here's something I recently did and didn't even realize I was doing it until later. One morning, I realized I had to make a phone call to a generally unpleasant person to straighten up a matter. I absolutely dreaded making the call. I put it off the whole day. I engaged in busy work, I made other phone calls, I filed some papers—but the whole time I had a knot in my stomach about what I knew I had to do.

Finally, it was late afternoon and I knew I couldn't put it off any longer. I finally just picked up the phone and made the call. To my surprise, it went well—far better than I had expected. I had wasted my whole day worrying, only for it to turn out fine. I was reminded of the book, *Eat That Frog*, in which Brian Tracy suggests you should do the most difficult task first and everything after that will be easier. It's true!

The whole day I lived in dread anticipation, worrying about that conversation. I couldn't even focus on the task at hand because, mentally, I was somewhere else the whole day. Do you find yourself doing that? You rob yourself of fully enjoying the present because while your body may be in the present, your mind isn't.

Consider this: Eighty percent of the things you worry about never happen, and the other twenty percent you have no control over. So why waste time worrying?

You can't go back and you can't go forward. Right now is all you have. If you do anything less than make the most of every second you have, you're living below your potential. You can live a better life just by doing more with what you already have!

Frequently, I meet people who say they don't have enough time to go after their dream, to write the book they've been thinking about, to gain the skills their changing industry requires, or to pursue an interest they've always had. When I hear those words, I think about a quote from H. Jackson Brown, Jr., author of *Life's Little Instruction Book*:

> *Don't say you don't have enough time. You have exactly the same number of hours per day that were given to Helen Keller, Pasteur, Michelangelo, Mother Teresa, Leonardo De Vinci, Thomas Jefferson, and Albert Einstein.*

How can you argue with that? We're all given the same amount of time. The difference is these people decided to seize the moments they were given and do something great!

As you go through your day, take a second to ask yourself where your mind is. Are you regretting the past, worrying about the future, or fully living in the present?

Be Aware of Your Time

Recently, I went back to the neighborhood where I grew up. I saw the old house. I saw what was left of the basketball backboard my dad built for me and my brothers still nailed to the tree. The familiar trees, the same streets—it brought back a lot of memories.

I saw my old trail going down to the lake where I used to go fishing. I saw myself walking down the trail, fishing pole in hand, kicking the dirt...and dreaming of what my life would become.

Where did all the time go?

Time is so short, and there's never enough of it for all you want to do. You have to prioritize your time for the things that are important to you. Time-management is self-management.

GOYA-ism:

**Learning to master time
is really learning to master yourself.**

If you're always late, get a day planner or set an alarm on your phone. As you become more aware of time, you'll become more respectful of the time you have. If you're always turning assignments in late, make a better plan— and then make yourself stick to it. If it seems that you never have enough time for the important things, find the time. Start planning. You'll be surprised how things fall into place once you're scheduling priorities.

Get off your attitude and live in the now!

GOYA-cise:

Take five minutes to plan tomorrow. Have a to-do list and a not-to-do list. Sometimes knowing what to say "no" to is just as important as what you say "yes" to. For the next week, keep a little notepad handy and quickly journal how you're spending your day; review it to see where you invest your time. Next, write yourself a check for how much you want to be worth in an hour of time. Tape the check where you'll see it from time to time. Ask yourself if you're spending your time working toward that income.

What you do with your time will decide your future. You won't be able to live in the now if you're still stuck in the past. You have to learn to deal with your past. You have to get past it.

Chapter 5

Get Past Your Past

Leave the past. Engage the present. Create the future. —Julio Melara

HAVE YOU EVER BEEN shot with a twelve-gauge shotgun? Believe me, it hurts.

On the last day of my junior year of high school, there were several parties; everyone wanted to have a good time. I showed up at a one of them where, unbeknownst to me, some guys from one school had just finished beating up some guys from another school. The guys who were beaten up left. My buddies and I arrived just before they returned to the party—with a shotgun.

They fired it into the air and everyone hit the ground trying to stay out of their way. I was scrambling to make sure a friend I was with didn't get hurt when I heard another shot....and felt the impact. One bullet passed completely through my chest. The other one I still have in my shoulder.

Even today, my doctors and I consider it a miracle that I wasn't killed. I thank God everyday that I wasn't.

I had had a brush with death. If the guy had been holding the shotgun a little differently, if he had been standing a bit closer....it's still a bit scary to think about. I had to undergo surgery, go to countless doctors, hospital visits, and months of rehabilitation. How do you think you would feel if all your friends spent their summer having a great time while you were going through physical therapy? I know how I felt, but I made up my mind I wasn't going to let this experience define me.

It happened, I dealt with it, and I moved on. Life's too short to live in the past!

What's in Your Past?

Sometimes I feel like there's an old movie reel in my head. When I'm feeling down or when I doubt my ability to face up to a challenge, I can hear it click on. It starts replaying all my failures, the hurtful words other people have said, the stupid things I've done, and all the missed opportunities I've had. It's like watching a movie of the worst parts of my life.

But I also try to remember the good times: times at the beach, traveling the country, spending fun summers with my grandmother, and hanging out with my friends. I have some amazing memories.

What about you? What's your life story? I'm sure you've had good times and bad times, too. There have been times you were happy to be alive and some days you'd like to forget altogether. There's nothing wrong with that—it's part of the human experience. The problem is allowing your past to determine your present and your future.

Your past is your history. You can't go back and change things, no matter how much you wish you could. You can't always be re-living the great times, either. It just doesn't work that way.

What you *can* do is change how you think about it. You can accept life for what it was in that moment but realize you have to live in the present. You don't have to let the past determine who you are right now. You can reinvent yourself any time you're ready.

Some people live in the past for different reasons. An acquaintance told me about a friend of his who wears his high school letter jacket even though he's in his thirties. For him, high school was his peak—the highlight of his life—and he's trying to go back.

What about you? Are you still wearing your version of a letter jacket? It's one thing to reminiscence; it's something completely differently to re-live past experiences, over and over.

Write down the experiences in your life you haven't gotten over yet. Decide what you need to do to come to peace with them. If it's counseling, get it. If you need to apologize, do it! You can't fully live until you've come to peace with your past.

Leave Your Baggage at the Station

One of my friend's bosses once told him: "One of my biggest headaches is that I have to suffer for the misdeeds of my employees' old bosses. After they quit or they were fired, they show up for work here, taking their anger and frustration out on me. For some reason, they expect me to do the same things their old boss did. The other guy made the mistake, but I'm the one who has to pay for it!"

Some people drag their past into the present all the time. I know several who had someone cheat on them, so they expected their next relationship to turn out the same way. There are business owners who have had a customer cheat them and then started treating the rest of their customers as if they'll do it, too.

Some people don't even realize the bitterness or grudges they continue to have—they're unaware of why they treat some people as they do.

You have to figure out what emotional baggage you're lugging around and leave it at the station. Carrying it with you only weighs you down and keeps you from boarding the train of life.

I was never considered the best and brightest student. I was just a B-C kind of guy. I had to take the college entrance exam three times to get in. I even had one high school teacher tell me I'd never amount to much. But I wasn't going to let that hold me down. I've moved on with my life. I'm not going to let my past be an anchor. I use it as a ladder to climb up. I believe everything happens for a reason. Right now, I could still be whining about the loss of my company and the abrupt detours in my life. THAT would be a miserable life!

You have a past, right? Things you'd love to change? Things you've done or things other people have done to you? You can't change it. The issue is your attitude about what happened. How do you let it affect you now?

Whatever memories or experiences there are, you have to make peace with them. If you won your high school championship, be proud of the fact—and move on with the rest of your life. If you've lived through a tragedy, you don't have to let it define you—it can simply be something you experienced.

Joyce Meyer was named by *Time Magazine* as one of the most influential evangelical leaders in the United States. You wouldn't have guessed she would have earned that distinction judging by her past. She was abused as a child and then as an adult, stole from her employer, and was absolutely miserable. But Joyce's determination enabled her to overcome her past and move to a life of ministry, inspiring millions of people.

GOYA-ism:

Failure is an opinion

Moving on includes getting over what you and what other people have done to you in your past. We all love to receive a compliment, but what sticks with us are the hurtful words people have said over the years. I may receive a hundred compliments, but they're all going to be drowned out by the one criticism.

You can't let other people's opinions of you keep you down. You get to choose your own life, regardless of what happened in the past and what others think of you. You can move on with your life, even if others don't believe you have or you can.

You don't have to bury your past—you just need to come to peace with it. When you speak about an experience, you can talk about the good that came out of it and how it helped you become who you are today.

If you can't speak positively about a situation, don't talk about it all. (If you need counseling, by all means, get it!) Try to accept your past for what it was and get ready to move on with the rest of your life.

Be cognizant of how your past experiences are affecting your life and the people around you. Are you engaging in a relationship based on a previous one? Are you punishing the wrong people for what someone else did?

Engage the Present and Create the Future

Finish every day and be done with it. You have done what you could. Some blunders and absurdities no doubt have crept in; forget them as soon as you can. Tomorrow is a new day; begin it well and serenely and with too high a spirit to be cumbered with your old nonsense. This day is all that is good and fair. It is too dear, with its hopes and invitations, to waste a moment on yesterdays. —Ralph Waldo Emerson

Some people have a bad habit of holding grudges. For me, every night the slate gets wiped clean, and another day begins. It's up to you to decide what you're going to do with today. Are you going to live in the past or are you going to live in the present? Will you let your past be your future, or will you decide to change your life's course?

You can't be positive about the present and future while focused on the past. Let go. Enjoy what you have today and what you will have tomorrow. Focus on your dreams and forget about the movie reel playing the collection of the worst of your life. Surround yourself with eagles who encourage you to live the life you've imagined. Believe in yourself and let others have faith in you.

Get past your past!

If I'm having a bad day, I like to say Groucho Marx's affirmation (yes, *that* Groucho Marx):

Each morning when I open my eyes I say to myself: I, not events, have the power to make me happy or unhappy today. I can choose which it shall be. Yesterday is dead, tomorrow hasn't arrived yet. I have just one day, today, and I'm going to be happy in it.

GOYA-cise:

Make a list of your biggest regrets. Have you made peace with your past and everything in it? Make a list of your biggest achievements. Are you using any of them as an excuse to keep from achieving more? Watch how you think and talk about the past. Do you speak positively about it? If not, find the good in every situation which will let you do so. Watch how you talk about your future. Are you allowing your past to define your future?

Once you get past your past, it's a lot easier to deal with the present. But if you're not careful, you can let present circumstances weigh you down as much as past experiences. Would you like to know what my master strategy is for dealing with adversity?

I just **SMILE.**

Chapter 6

JUST SMILE

*The expression one wears on one's face is far
more important than the clothes one wears on
one's back.* —Dale Carnegie

HAD THE CHANCE to fulfill a lifetime wish—to hear
Tony Bennett sing "Smile." I have loved that song for
years and had always wanted to see him perform in person. I had four or five opportunities, but something always
came up. Finally, I was able to see him perform in New
Orleans at the Mahalia Jackson Theater. After all these
years, I couldn't believe I was going to hear my favorite
singer perform my favorite song!

My girlfriend and I took our seats in the balcony. I
could hardly keep still—it seemed surreal. Then the lights
dimmed and the spotlight hit him. A few songs in, he
started singing:

Smile though your heart is aching,
Smile even though it's breaking,
When there are clouds in the sky, you'll get by.

If you smile through your pain and sorrow,
Smile and maybe tomorrow,
You'll see the sun come shining through for you.

Light up your face with gladness,
Hide every trace of sadness,
Although a tear may be ever so near,

That's the time you must keep on trying.
Smile, what's the use of crying?
You'll find that life is still worthwhile,
If you just smile.

That song has gotten me through more rough days and bad times than anything else. It reminds me to just smile, in spite of whatever happens. You know who originally wrote the song? It was the master of all comedians, Charlie Chaplin.

The song talks about tears and trying to remember life is still worth living. How could such a melancholy song be written by a comedian? The truth is Charlie's life was anything but a comedy. His father was an alcoholic he barely knew who died from cirrhosis when Charlie was twelve. His mother suffered from a mental illness and was committed to an asylum while he was still young, and he wound up in a school for poor orphans. How did he become one of the most famous actors and creative geniuses of his time? He did what he wrote about—he smiled, in spite of what had happened in his life.

That's why the song holds so much meaning for me. No matter how bad life gets, I can smile and immediately feel better.

Why Smile?

Life isn't fair. Not even close. It's hard. There are times you wonder, "Why is everything bad happening to me?" When I lost my business and my income almost overnight, I felt horrible. When my dad was diagnosed with cancer, I felt it was unfair to him and my family. It was hard on all of us.

I could have wondered why these things were happening. But I knew that wouldn't solve anything. That would just make things worse. I had to force myself to smile, even though I didn't feel like it. I didn't want to be happy and cheery. But I smiled—and it made life a little easier.

It didn't change what was going on around me, but it changed the way I looked at it. Instead of coming at it with a why-me mentality, I tried to look on the bright side of things. If there wasn't a bright side, I tried to make the best of it.

People come to me and say, "But Ryan, you don't understand what's going on in my life. You have no idea how bad it is."

That's exactly the time when I tell them to smile, to put on a brave face and keep going, and try to make the best of a bad situation. You know what a smile really changes? It changes your attitude toward the situation.

A smile relaxes you and helps you find a place where you can deal positively with the curve ball life has thrown you. A smile reminds you that you have a choice of how you're going to let life affect you. Are you going to react with negative emotions and actions, or are you going to respond maturely and deal with the problem on your own terms? It's your choice. Make it positive.

Smiling changes more than just your attitude. Studies show that people who smile more are generally healthier and live longer. Did you know women usually live about five years longer than men? It's no coincidence that studies show women smile more often than men.

One time, I was having an all-around bad day when my girlfriend, Ann Marie, quoted from the movie, *Steel Magnolias*:

Smile! It increases your face value.

GOYA-ism:

Don't let your situation determine your attitude. Determining your attitude will change the situation!

What's Stopping You From Smiling?

Why aren't you smiling at least some of the time?

Is there something going on in your life, like an illness or money problems? Is it your spouse or some other loved one? Is it your job?

The real answer is that nothing's keeping you from smiling. You can smile any time you want to. Go ahead and try it right now…not a fake smile—do it for real. Treat yourself to a warm, genuine smile. Doesn't that feel great? You made one simple choice and it changed the way you felt.

You're wired to feel better when you smile. It's your natural emotional response. The simple act puts you in a better mood, no matter what else is going on around you. It's the same in choosing to have a positive attitude. It makes you feel better and puts you in a stronger frame of mind to deal with your problems.

Not too long ago, I attended an Irish wake for my best friend's dad and had the chance to see the effects of a person who chose to smile his whole life. For a big part of his life, the man was in a wheelchair due to multiple sclerosis. At the wake, I listened to his friends and family talk about his life, and they all said the same thing—you never heard him complain. He was one of the nicest, most cheerful people you'd ever meet. He didn't let his lack of mobility keep him from having a great attitude and from enriching the lives of those around him. He chose to smile in spite of his condition and lived a fulfilling life.

You have the same choice. The song asks, "What's the use of crying?" Are you going to cry and moan about your life—or are you going to smile?

What Makes You Smile?

I'll tell you what makes me smile—my niece and nephews. When I have a crummy day, I just swing by their house on the way home or give them a call. Their laughter and smiles are infectious. I can't help but feel great after being around them for a few minutes. I make sure I see them at least once or twice a week to get a refill on smiles.

What about you? What makes you smile? I hope you're like me and have family that makes you smile. But what else makes you smile? Do you have a hobby or something that helps you relax? Does a good movie make you laugh? How about reminiscing with an old friend?

Smiling is a choice, and it's a lot easier to make that choice if you're surrounded by things that make you smile. As you're surrounding yourself with positive influences, surround yourself with things that make you laugh. Hang around fun people, watch funny movies, and read books that put a smile on your face. It's easy to get sucked into other people's drama of watching negative shows and finding all the ways to be unhappy. But it's more productive to be around things that make you happy—not to mention a lot more fun.

People have told me they've enjoyed hearing me speak, enjoyed my enthusiasm, and that I've given them valuable information to use in their life and business. Do you think the effect would be the same if I had done the entire presentation looking unhappy?

What would you think if you were at one of my seminars and I frowned the whole time? Would you be as receptive? Would you get the same value out of the seminar? No way.

People are drawn to a smile. When you see someone with a warm, honest smile, you can't help but feel better yourself. Smiling is good for you and for everyone around you. I wish everyone smiled all the time. It would make the whole world a nicer place to live.

But people think they're trapped by circumstances. I know exactly what feeling stuck feels like. When I started chasing my dream of being a speaker and writing a book, some days I could see what life was going to be like— speaking in front of an audience, helping people, giving people tools to make their jobs and lives easier. If I had one of those days where I could see my dream coming to life, the next day I would get a cold, hard dose of reality.

I would remember all the nearly impossible tasks I had to take care of for my regular job and everything I had to do to make my dreams come true. Sometimes, it would feel like it was impossible. Every two steps forward seemed to end in three steps back. Some days it felt like I'd never get out of the hole I was in.

When you're feeling like that and get stuck, just smile. It immediately puts you in a better frame of mind to deal with the problem. Remember, that's exactly *"the time you must keep on trying."*

Share Your Smile

My close friend Ryan Maranto has an enthusiastic, outgoing personality. He's just one of those great people you want to be around. He always has something positive to say, he's always full of energy, and he's always smiling.

We were good friends for a year before I found out he had previously had cancer. Can you believe that? A whole year we were around each other, talking and hanging out before I ever knew he had beaten cancer earlier in his life. He never mentioned it. I would never have known had another friend not told me.

I asked how he got through such a hard time, especially at such a young age. Do you know what he said? He just stayed positive throughout the whole ordeal—from finding out he had cancer, during the cancer treatment, and now on the other side of it all, he just stayed positive. He just smiled.

I've met people who whine about something as simple as a hangnail—nothing life-threatening—but you would think they were going to meet their maker tomorrow. They bellyached about it and talked about how bad it was non-stop.

I'm not making light of anyone's medical problems, but do you see the contrast there? I was close friends with someone for a year before I ever knew he had faced his mortality.

GOYA-ism:

You can't smile if you have a mouthful of problems.

You come across these people all the time. Instead of spitting out their problems, they chew on them like an old piece of gum. The lesson is that the sooner you spit out your problems, the sooner you'll get past them. You'll be happier, and so will everyone around you.

You see, a smile doesn't just benefit you—it's for people around you, too. Just like my nieces and nephews put a smile on my face, I want to be the person that puts a smile on others' faces. It could be in a seminar, having coffee with a friend, or in something I write. I want to be the person other people want to be around.

Make a habit of smiling at everyone, even on the phone. Believe it or not, people can hear you smile!

SMILE!

Smiling doesn't mean you pretend everything's going right. Smiling is a choice to find the positive in every adverse situation and to deal with it in a mature way. Here is the acronym I created for smile:

Stop and think
Measure the problem
Identify solutions
Live and learn
Enjoy the outcome

First, don't react. Don't be emotionally trigger-happy. Pause to think about what just happened.

Second, measure the problem. How big is it? Is it something that will blow over in a few minutes that you don't even need to waste your time on? Or is part of a much larger issue that needs to be addressed?

Third, get out of your mental rut. Don't necessarily go with your first instinct. Think and find positive solutions to the issue and engage them as an emotionally mature adult.

Fourth, look at the problem as a learning experience. You survived and you can always learn something to make yourself better. What did you learn from this situation?

Fifth and last, once you've decided to smile, enjoy the outcome. Give yourself time to recover before leaping into something else. Come to a place where you're at peace and you can truly smile at the situation.

If you are distressed by anything external, the pain is not due to the thing itself, but to your estimate of it; and this you have the power to revoke at any moment. —Marcus Aurelius

I wake up every morning and say, "Okay life, what interesting opportunities do you have for me today?" That's my way to prepare for the difficulties in life. I'm not some crazy guy who enjoys the bad times—I know they'll make me a stronger, better person.

I believe there are no coincidences—everything happens for a reason. Everyone's faced with obstacles in life. The question is how do you deal with it? We're conditioned to look at difficulties and problems in a negative light. I challenge you to look at them instead as growing opportunities.

For example, if the insurance company I was a partner in had flourished, I would still be the vice president of sales instead of pursuing my dream of being a motivational speaker and author. The terrible circumstances of life were actually the start of me rediscovering and pursuing my passion.

We all go through seasons in our lives. For me, starting over in Baton Rouge and taking an entry-level sales job was hard to swallow. But I kept smiling, knowing "this, too, shall pass." Maybe you're going through a season in your life where everything seems bleak and dreary. Maybe you've fallen on hard times. I don't know your situation, but I do know how you feel.

Believe me, smiling a real smile when you don't feel like it is one of the hardest things to do—but it's one of the best things you can do. And don't just smile—SMILE!

If you wait for life to be perfect before you start smiling, you never will. Things will never be absolutely perfect. But if you'll smile, *"you'll find that life is still worthwhile."*

GOYA-cise:

Get a copy of "Smile." Tony Bennett's version is my favorite, but Nat King Cole, Josh Groban, Michael Bublé, and dozens of others have their own versions. Find your favorite artist and listen to it until you can sing it to yourself. Make sure the next time you're faced with a challenge; you'll look at it in a mature way. Then, just SMILE

Smiling at life is one key ingredient in getting off your attitude. Another is faith. You not only have to believe things will work out—you have to act in faith.

Chapter 7

ACT IN FAITH

A man of courage is also full of faith.
—Marcus Tullius Cicero

WHAT IS FAITH? You hear about it. You read about it. But what is it?

One dictionary defines faith as "a confident belief in the truth, value, or trustworthiness of a person, an idea, or a thing; a belief that does not rest on logical proof or material evidence."

Do you want to know what faith really is? It's an action.

One of the best examples I've ever heard explaining faith is the one about the African impala. This little animal is only about three feet tall, but it can jump nine feet vertically and over thirty feet horizontally. This is the kicker—you can keep an impala in a small pen only four feet high and the impala will never escape. It's capable—it has the ability and the means to do so—but it stays confined in its tiny pen. Why? Because the impala lives by sight—it won't jump if it can't see where it will land.

We're the same way. We live our whole lives in tiny cages because we can't see where we'll land if we try to escape. We live by sight. Faith, on the other hand, acts without knowing the outcome. You jump and then figure out where you're going to land.

Faith is a key ingredient in creating a positive attitude and lifestyle. You can't do it without faith. Faith is the glue that holds you together when, by all accounts, you should be shaken apart. Faith in God is what keeps you going when everything's falling down around you. Faith in yourself and faith in others is what ties all of us together and makes life worth living.

The opposite of faith is fear and doubt. When you doubt, you don't believe things are going to work out, that the worst will happen, and that everything will fall apart. You could say it this way—doubt is negative belief. Faith, on the other hand, is positive belief.

The funny thing is, either way you go, you believe in something that hasn't happened yet. Both are just mindsets or attitudes.

I'll never forget waiting at the hospital while my dad underwent surgery for cancer. I kept thinking about all the things that could go wrong. What if the surgeon was just a little tired? What if someone's hand slipped? What if—?

Finally, I had to stop myself. I had to have faith in the doctors and believe that everything would turn out okay. It wasn't easy. Imagine if it were your parent on the operating table. It's a hard situation to accept. I had to choose to be optimistic about the outcome or to be pessimistic about the possibilities. I chose optimistic faith.

Knowing the surgeon's success rate didn't help. Knowing that the statistics favored my dad didn't help. No facts or figures could have made me feel better about my dad undergoing surgery. Ultimately, it was just an emotional decision to believe in the best.

What about you? Have you ever faced a situation where you simply had to trust that things were going to be okay? Maybe you have had money problems, or a loved one who had an accident, or you were facing a fork in the road of life. I don't know what's going on in your life at this time. But I do know that having faith has helped me through the darkest times in my own life.

Take the first step in faith. You don't have to see the whole staircase, just take the first step. —Dr. Martin Luther King, Jr.

What Does Faith Look Like?

Faith is an integral part of your attitude—you can't see it or touch it, but you can see its effect. You can also see its absence.

People who don't have faith in anything are some of the most miserable and fearful people you'll ever meet. They don't have faith in themselves and never achieve anything. They don't have faith in other people and always believe others are trying to cheat them. They don't have faith in God or life, and are always expecting the worst.

On the other hand, people who have faith are positive about the future. They believe in the basic goodness of humankind. They're confident in what they can accomplish and they feel great about life.

They're two totally different people, but all that really separates them is whether they've chosen to have a positive or negative belief about the way things are.

One of the most inspiring stories I've seen unfold before my eyes is the story of Drew Brees, the quarterback who took the New Orleans Saints to their first-ever Super Bowl victory. Drew was playing for the San Diego Chargers when he hurt his shoulder and the team let him go. He was in talks with the Miami Dolphins, but they decided not to take the risk that his shoulder wouldn't heal. He finally signed with the Saints. A few seasons later, he led the team to their first Super Bowl and beat the Indianapolis Colts 31-17.

Drew had to have faith in himself the whole time, even while medical professionals expressed no confidence in his ability to play. He had faith in his team, even though they had never been to the Super Bowl. He also maintained his faith in God, believing that difficult things in his life would end in success. He kept trusting and believing— and it paid off.

In his book *Coming Back Stronger,* Drew talked about his acronym of FAITH. The "A" stood for attitude. According to Drew, you can't always determine your circumstances, but you can always determine your attitude. That's how he sees faith—it's based, in part, on your attitude.

Drew is someone I look up to and draw inspiration from. This guy led my hometown football team to the Super Bowl, on sheer faith. Wow! If I act in faith, what kind of great things will I see come to pass in my life? Will my faith and my life be the instrument to help other people achieve their dreams? I hope so.

Drew's story highlights three important areas you must have faith in if you want to achieve a positive lifestyle— faith in God, faith in yourself, and faith in others. What are some perfect examples from your life that illustrate the importance of faith in each of those areas?

Have a Spiritual Faith

I'm not telling you where to find your spiritual faith—but I will tell you that you must have it. Your attitude is affected and, in many cases, determined by your spiritual faith. If you don't have any kind of trust that life's events somehow make sense or are leading toward something, you go through life believing it's just a series of random events and human decisions. Can you see how pessimistic that outlook is?

One of my favorite passages from the Bible defines faith:

For we walk by faith, not by sight. —2 Corinthians 5:7 (NKJV)

I don't believe there are coincidences in life. There have been too many doors opened; too many opportunities laid out in front of me, for me to believe they were all random coincidences.

For example, while living in Baton Rouge, several friends told me I needed to meet Julio Melara, an accomplished businessman and speaker. I tried a few times to meet him, but it never seemed to happen. Surprisingly, one Sunday, when I was attending my family's church in Mandeville, Louisiana, the pastor introduced his friend Julio. Finally there was my chance to meet him. Not too long after that, he invited me to come speak at his company.

As I do at every event, I took pictures at his company for my website and my marketing material.

Almost a year later, I posted a compilation video on Facebook of my seminars and people wearing my *Get Off Your Attitude* bracelet. I tagged everyone in the video, including Julio. A publisher was looking over Julio's Facebook page and saw my video. The publisher approached me about publishing this book—just after I had signed a contract with the editor that my friend Jim recommended to me. The funny thing is Jim lives in Dallas, Texas and the editor he found for me lives in Baton Rouge, Louisiana—a short drive down the interstate from me.

In three months, I went from being discouraged somewhat about ever having this book completed to finding the right editor, signing with a publisher, and having the book finished. Can you see how a string of random events resulted in one of my dreams being fulfilled? Can you really call that coincidence?

Albert Einstein said:

Coincidence is God's way of remaining anonymous.

I put my faith in God. As you've read, there was a time in my life when I was on the wrong path, making choices which could have completely altered my future. But somewhere along that path, I came to believe I had a greater purpose than the life I was living. My spiritual faith healed me and brought me to the place I am now.

There were plenty of times my spiritual faith kept me out of dark places, as if I was a child and God was yanking me back from running out into the street.

Once I renewed my spiritual faith and got in sync with my purpose in life, doors started flying open for me. The same is, or will be, true for you. Once you've discovered your spiritual purpose and have aligned yourself with it, opportunities will start appearing out of nowhere.

When I feel stressed and anxious, I know my faith is low. I pray and remind myself what I'm supposed to be doing. It always makes me feel better and renews my confidence. I encourage you to somehow find your own spiritual faith and let it strengthen and renew you.

Have Faith in Yourself

You absolutely must have faith in yourself if you're going to create a great life and live it to the fullest. What do I mean by that? You have to believe that you're better than what you see right now—that you have incredible, untapped potential. If you're unhappy with what you've done or become, believe you can do more and be more.

You also have to believe you can achieve the dream you've envisioned. I could list dozens or hundreds of inspiring stories about people who believed in themselves, even when no one else would. In fact, almost every great story you read or you hear has some part where the person had to keep their dream alive even while the odds were against them.

People who don't believe in themselves are some of the most depressing, pessimistic, pitiful individuals you'll ever meet. They don't think they can achieve anything, so they never try. They're defined by their failures.

Doubt is a natural human emotion. Every time I get up to speak, I hear little whispers in my mind. "Who do you think you are to speak to people?" Every time I think about this book, I hear doubt say, "Who are you to write a book telling people to get off their attitude?" But I continue to act in faith, believing in my purpose and my ability. Believe in yourself and others will have faith in you, too.

If you don't have faith in yourself, remember the times you've been proud of yourself. Think about when you did the right thing, made a good choice, or helped someone else. Don't dwell on your failures—remember the great things you've accomplished, however small or however long ago.

GOYA-ism:

**People won't have faith in you,
until you have faith in yourself.**

Have Faith in Others

I would never have had the courage to reach my dreams if it hadn't been for other people believing in me. I owe so much to Ann Marie. We met shortly after I decided to pursue this book. There were plenty of days when I just wanted to give up, but she wouldn't let me.

She would say, "Ryan, I believe you can achieve the dreams God has set out for you. I know you can!"

Do you know what that did for me? Do you have any idea how much that meant to me? to know someone had that kind of faith in me? Her words inspired me to get out of my self-pity and act in faith.

Think about your life. Someone has let you down before, haven't they? They disappointed you, they betrayed you, and they used you. It doesn't matter—you still have to have faith in other people. Have you ever disappointed yourself? You still have to go on having faith in yourself. It's the same thing with others—you have to have faith in them, even when they give you a reason not to.

Another way you have faith in others is in our human systems; for example: police, firemen, teachers, and government officials. We have to have a certain amount of faith in these systems or we'd have a total breakdown in society. Do you know someone who believes every conspiracy theory that comes out? Do they live a successful, happy life? No—they're always full of fear, anger, and suspicion.

Sometimes our leaders and officials mess up. You mess up. I mess up. But when it happens, it's not one strike and you're out. If that were the case, I would have been out of the game a long time ago. But even while I was messing up, people still had faith in me—and that faith inspired me to live a better life.

In "Get Past Your Past," you made a list of things that have previously happened in your life. Is there anyone on that list you need to forgive or to whom you can give a second chance? Is there someone in your life right now who needs to be reminded you have faith in them?

GOYA-ism:

**Fear and doubt keep the doors of life closed.
Faith is what kicks those doors open.**

Kick in Your Faith

There is a direct connection between faith and attitude. The more faith you have—spiritually, personally, and in others—the more positive you'll be. When you've messed up, when people let you down, and when life is going wrong—that's the best time to kick your faith into overdrive. You're not living in denial. You're continuing to move forward confidently.

One of the shortest and best ways I've ever seen faith explained was told to me by my friend Amber. She said,

"Here's how faith works:

Believe, apply, receive. Repeat."

That's faith. You believe, you act, and then you achieve! Kick in your faith with whatever you're doing in life! Don't wait until you've done some great things before you start believing in yourself—believe in yourself right now! Don't wait until people prove themselves to you—have faith which inspires people to achieve great things! And don't wait until life unfolds perfectly—have faith in your spiritual purpose.

Faith isn't something you feel—it's something you do!

GOYA-cise:

Go find your spiritual faith. Talk to someone whose spiritual faith you admire and who seems to know their purpose. Have faith in yourself. List all the things you've ever done that you were proud of or happy about. Reflect on this list when you doubt yourself. Make a list of people who have let you down, but try to find something good about each of them. Have faith in others.

As you've seen, attitude is mostly in your head. It's mainly a battle in your mind of getting past the negativity and focusing on the positive. But now it's time to talk about your body—one of the biggest factors in achieving and maintaining a positive attitude.

Chapter 8

HAVE A WEALTH OF HEALTH

The first wealth is health.
—Ralph Waldo Emerson

ONE OF THE BEST THINGS about my getting shot was going through physical therapy.

While that may not sound like much fun to you, it opened my eyes to the importance of health and wellness. It's what prompted me to study sports medicine at the University of Southern Mississippi and helped me develop healthy habits I plan to have all my life. Because of my focus on health, I had the opportunity to write a series of "mental fitness" articles in a local health and wellness publication. For one article, I interviewed Mackie Shilstone. He inspired me to re-examine the importance of health in creating a positive lifestyle.

If you don't know who Mackie Shilstone is, he is one of the pioneers of the health and fitness industry. He's trained over 3,000 athletes and celebrities such as John Goodman, Riddick Bowe, Serena Williams, Michael Spinks, Bernard Hopkins, Steve Wynn, and Ozzie Smith, not to mention the Giants, the Blues, and about half of the Cardinals. He was voted one of the fifty most influential people in the history of boxing and is a special advisor to the U.S. Olympic Committee.

All of that is impressive—but that's not the main thing which inspired me. He said two things which have stuck with me since then. The first was:

There are no excuses. None!

To illustrate his point, he told me about watching a college football team run track before the start of their summer conditioning program. He thought they were lazy. He challenged them to fourteen-minute conditioning drills and almost half the team couldn't keep up with him. You might say, "Okay Ryan, the guy stays in shape. What's the big deal?" This is the big deal: Mackie Shilstone was more that twice their age! There are no excuses!

Here's the second thing he said which stays with me: "I tell everyone there are no barriers between the average person and a million-dollar athlete…only different goals and training times." In other words, they have a different attitude toward the level of their commitment and achievement. After working with thousands of top performers, Mackie knows what he's talking about!

There's no way I could write a book about attitude and not talk about health. A healthy attitude and a healthy body go hand in hand. You can't affect one without affecting the other. What am I talking about? Here are a few examples from well-researched studies:

- Exercise improves your mood
- Exercise lowers stress levels
- People with a positive self-image are more likely to eat right and exercise
- On average, people who regularly exercise have higher self-esteem (and higher incomes)

Do you see how one affects the other? They're strongly linked. If you want one, you have to have the other.

Do you like your body? Unfortunately, you would probably answer "no." You see your ideal image in a fitness magazine and immediately want to lose weight, wish your hair were a different color, or want to change something else about yourself. One of the first steps in being healthy is accepting yourself as you are. Overall, how you were made is the same as your past—you can't change it. All you can do is go from here.

At one time, I was made fun of because of my looks and my height. I'm not a tall guy. But going through my whole life wishing I were taller would be a waste of time, energy, and emotion. I've accepted I'm not tall and that's how I was made. That's it.

The first step in getting healthy is to accept yourself as you are. Don't beat yourself up.

GOYA-ism:

Accept the things you can't change and focus on improving the things you can.

Get Positive by Being Healthy

You can't change how you were made but you can change how you treat your body. One of my good friends is Steve Jordan, "America's Fitness Ambassador." He told me an inspiring story about Brenda, a client of his. She was 5 feet 4 inches and 53 years old. She had considered herself fat ever since her childhood. Consequently, she didn't take care of her body like she should have. But at some point, she told herself, "Enough is enough."

She started working out with Steve and began to manage her diet, sleep, stress levels, and her overall lifestyle. In a short span of time, she reached her goal weight of 115 pounds—a number her scale hadn't seen since she was in second grade!

This is a perfect example of someone who decided to get off her attitude and do something about her health.

You know what the biggest benefit for Brenda was? It was the positive energy she felt from feeling good in her body and in her spirit. People complimented her on how well she looked, but people also started talking about the new aura around her. She was projecting a confidence—a radiance, you could say—she never had before. Not only did she love her body, but she was more in love with her life!

Don't you want to be like Brenda? The truth is there's no difference between people like her and people like you. You can do it! Find some areas in your life where you can make a healthier choice. Watch how feeling healthier makes you feel better.

Get Healthy by Being Positive

I was once told by a friend, "You know, there's no way I would let other people say to me what I say to myself. I wouldn't let other people call me fat or ugly, but that's what I call myself all day long."

Maybe you don't have a shot at being Miss America or Mr. Universe, but that's no reason to put yourself down. Be positive about your self-image. If you want to lose weight, don't tell yourself you're fat. You don't have to be in denial—just acknowledge you're not at the weight you want to be, but you're working toward a healthier you. If you want to run for three minutes without gasping for breath, don't beat yourself up over how out of shape you are. Smile about it and stay focused on getting in shape.

I just told you the story about Brenda. Now let me tell you about Steve Jordan, the guy who trained her. In 1994, Steve fell off of a balcony at Johns Hopkins University. The fall was nearly fatal. As it was, Steve had to have emergency brain surgery. The trauma to his head injured his spinal cord, his brain, his facial muscles, and even his short-term memory. He was in the hospital and rehab for months undergoing reconstructive surgery, therapy, and learning how to take care of himself again.

Steve decided not to let his condition keep him from enjoying life. He returned to class despite the looks he got from others staring at his scars, noticing his facial deformities, and listening to his unfocused speech. With dedication and determination, Steve was able to overcome his hardships and became one of the world's foremost experts on health and fitness. He has worked with the White House Athletic Center and has appeared on talk shows and in magazines throughout the country.

Steve told me it was his positive mindset that kept him focused and motivated through his rehabilitation. I think his story is inspiring because it tells you that you can achieve your health goals by starting with the right attitude.

Once you're living a generally positive lifestyle, use your newly-found confidence to take on bigger challenges in your health.

Invest in Your Body

Do you believe in working smarter, not harder? Obviously it's the smart thing to do, right?

Abraham Lincoln once said if he had six hours to chop down a tree, he'd spend the first five hours sharpening the axe. In other words, he would invest time upfront to make the actual work go much faster. You can do the same thing in your life by investing in your health. If you'll spend time being healthier, you'll be able to do everything else better.

When I work out, I sleep better. I wake up refreshed; I'm in a great state of mind and ready to tackle the day's challenges. At the end of the day, I don't feel so exhausted. In fact, I still have enough energy left over to hit the gym and start the cycle all over again. When I take care of my body, my body takes care of me.

Those who think they have not time for bodily exercise will sooner or later have to find time for illness. —Edward Stanley, Earl of Derby

Find time to be healthy!

Being healthier:

- Gives you more energy
- Makes you more productive
- Helps you focus on your work
- Keeps you emotionally balanced (think of how you act when you're tired)
- Keeps you from getting sick as often

- Extends your life (on average, by 7.8 years)
- Puts things in perspective. (Problems don't seem so bad after a good night's sleep.)
- Helps you manage stress
- Helps you get more out of life and have more fun!

When you exercise, your body releases endorphins—hormones which naturally make you feel better. Sure, physical activity wears you out, but endorphins are the reward your body gives itself. Endorphins lower your stress, raise your energy, and improve your mood.

You need to have a healthy body just as you need to have a healthy attitude. They're both the foundation on which you build everything else. If you have bad health, it's a lot harder to do everything else, isn't it? Think about the effects of being unhealthy. You have less energy, so you don't feel like accomplishing as much. If you never get enough sleep, you're always operating at a sub-optimal level. If you don't get the nutrition you need, you won't stay healthy.

When you think about it, it's a no-brainer. It's just smart to make healthy choices. Have I always made healthy choices, even after being enrolled in a sports medicine program? No. I've made some not-so-healthy decisions—some that were even out of character at the time I made them. But at some point, I realized what I was doing, and I made a decision to distance myself from those choices. I'm too focused on my goals and I respect my body too much.

I know where I'm going, and I know I need a healthy body to get me there.

Make your health a priority. See a doctor; get a trainer; get on an exercise regimen and stick to it!

Your Health Starts With Your Attitude

I read an article in *USA Today* in which a psychology professor was talking about how high levels of psychological well-being benefit your health. The researcher said there is evidence that a positive attitude isn't only a state of mind—it also affects what physically happens in your brain and body. In fact, some researchers are now saying that having a positive mental attitude is one of the very best things you can do for your health!

> *"Being in a good frame of mind helps keep one in the picture of health."* – Author unknown

It makes sense when you think about it. Your body responds to your emotions. For me, public speaking is something I love to do; for others, the very thought makes their heart beat faster.

When you're afraid, your body reacts with the "fight or flight" instinct. Your body doesn't know it's not a life or death situation—all it knows is that it's getting bad signals from the brain, and so it gets your body ready for action. If you're constantly in a state of panic, your body will stay tense and keyed up. It's like running your car at full throttle—a little bit is okay, but you can't keep it up forever. We're just not built for that.

But you can change. If you're in a relaxed frame of mind, your body can relax. If you go to sleep without anxiety, you rest better. If you don't live in a state of fear all the time, your body can focus on healing itself instead of staying tensed for a fight.

The bottom line is this:

GOYA-ism:

**Once you decide to be healthier,
a positive attitude is the best place to start!**

Just Do It!

I hear people say, "Well, I just don't have enough time to go to the gym. I have kids, and a house, and a job—I just don't have time!" As we talked about in "Get on With It"—you do have time for the things that are important. Get up an hour earlier and exercise while the kids are asleep. Go ahead and listen to an inspirational podcast while you're at it. Twice a week, take your lunch break to walk for thirty minutes.

Start making small changes in other places in your life. Start skipping a fast food run and grab something healthy instead. Order the tuna steak instead of the beef steak. Go ahead and park in the middle of the parking lot instead of circling it three times looking for a space up front. (You'll spend about the same amount of time.)

You have time to eat healthier. You have time to exercise. You have time to make better choices about your body. Stop making excuses and just do it!

GOYA-cise:

Keep a food journal for a few days to see how much you're consuming. Don't try to tackle the world all at once. Make small but healthier choices. Go get your annual check-up. Commit to some kind of physical routine, even if it's only ten minutes of walking per day.

Health is the first wealth, as Emerson said. Now that you have a better attitude toward your health, let's talk about what wealth usually means—money.

Chapter 9

MAKE MONEY, DO GOOD

*If a person gets his attitude toward money
straight, it will help straighten out almost
every other area in his life.* —Billy Graham

WAS NEVER GOOD with money. At least, that's what I told
myself. I didn't even trust myself with money. You would
think because my parents were successful businesspeo-
ple, I would have learned how to value and respect money.
To their credit, they tried to teach me—but with me, it was
in one ear and out the other.

I was at spring break when I signed up for my first
credit card in order to get a free t-shirt. I quickly fell into
the credit trap and racked up credit card debt I couldn't
pay. Even well into my adult life, I still hadn't figured out
how to handle my money. I even had my condo foreclosed
on. Ouch!

As of right now, I'm still paying for my ignorance and mistakes. I've learned the hard way to get my attitude toward money straight—and I'm still learning. But all the times people have helped me when I was going through tough times changed my attitude toward money. I want to be in a position where I am one of those people who have the money to help other people.

One of my favorite quotes about money is by one of the authors of the *Chicken Soup for the Soul* series. He said:

The best way to help the poor is to not be one of them. — Mark Victor Hansen

When some people hear me quote that, they cringe. But think about it—if you're poor, you can't help yourself ,and you certainly can't help other people. The way you put yourself in a position to not be a burden, but a boost to others, is to be financially secure. If you manage to be wealthy—well, so much the better.

But discussions about being wealthy or poor always seem to stir up controversy. The subject of money sparks all kinds of debate. People have some deep-set perspectives and old wounds when it comes to money. Whether it's a divorce, childhood fears about poverty, fights over who's making the most—all of that boils down to money. To a large degree, money affects your relationships, your decisions, and your life. Wouldn't you agree?

But you know what? It's really not money that affects these areas of your life. It's your attitude toward money.

Money isn't a good thing, but it's not a bad thing, either. In fact, money isn't anything more than a tool for you to use. All the hype and obsession with money is really over how people deal with money. Some people use it for good. Some people use it for bad. Some people don't know how to use it at all.

Where Do You Get Your Attitude Toward Money?

Have you seen the 1987 movie *Wall Street* with Michael Douglas playing the ruthless Wall Street trader, Gordon Gekko? Most people I meet remember this one particular line:

The point is, ladies and gentlemen, that greed, for lack of a better word, is good.

Here are the three different responses I hear to that quote:

1. "See that? That's what money does to you! It brings out the worst in people!"

2. "Greed is good! Right on!"

3. "Yeah, it must be nice to have money. But I guess just getting by is okay."

These three types of people all have different attitudes about money. One thinks it's evil, one idolizes Gordon

Gekko, and the third group sits around and says, "Must be nice." All three mentalities are wrong.

Think about specifically who or what influenced your attitude about money. Has someone taken time to really teach you about it, or have your lessons just been from popular culture and bad experiences?

Is Money Evil?

Do you think money is evil?

Friends will ask me, "Doesn't the Bible say money is the root of all evil?"

No. It says the *love* of money is the root of all evil. In other words, your attitude toward money is the problem—not money itself. If you'll read the verses in the Bible dealing with wealthy people, it's their spirit the scriptures condemn—not their money.

It seems to me the people who have this mindset want to be self-righteous and pretend they're above the petty needs of money. This was the attitude of the aristocratic rich in Medieval Europe. It was impolite to talk about money; merchants, traders, and people who dealt with money were the lower classes.

In her book *Winning in Life Now,* my friend Michelle Prince said it like this:

Make Money, Do Good

"I felt guilty if I was successful, and especially if I made a lot of money. I had a negative idea of what "rich" people were like: snotty, arrogant, aloof, and alone. I didn't want to have any of those traits, so subconsciously I thought, 'I don't want to be rich.'"

Michelle gained a better perspective on money, but the group who still holds this view believes that the wealthy are people who came by their money dishonestly—that they somehow lied, cheated, and stole to get to the top. They also believe there is some kind of virtue in being broke. In other words, poor people are good and wealthy people are bad.

If you've lived in reality for any amount of time, you know that's not true. Many wealthy people have done great things. Andrew Carnegie, Bill Gates, and Warren Buffet have given billions of dollars to charities. Some people have done awful things, like Bernie Madoff.

I'm using the term "wealthy" instead of "rich," because you don't have to have money to have the real riches in life: love, friendships, memories, etc.

Some poor people also do great things. Many help others even when they don't have much money themselves.

Some people have committed crimes too horrible to even think about. It's not how much they had in their bank account that decided whether they did good or bad. It was their choice in life.

Is Greed Good?

I've never identified with those people who believe money is bad. I'm the guy who dropped out of college to go chase money. Even after I went back to college and graduated, I went back to chasing money. I wanted to get into the thick of things again. I knew I was going places, and it didn't matter what I had to sacrifice to get there. It wasn't until years later I discovered you don't chase money—you *attract* it.

In traveling and living around the country, I've met some people who were absolutely fanatical about money. For these types, everyone around them was a rung on their ladder to success. They approached people with the mindset of, "What can you do for me?" They were the true embodiment of Gekko's motto that greed is good. For them, money is a way to keep score; whoever has the most, wins.

The problem with these people is they miss the whole point in life. What's the sense in having money if you've traded your integrity, your values, and even your relationships for a few bucks?

I like how Dave Ramsey put it in *The Total Money Makeover*:

> *We buy things we don't need with money we don't have to impress people we don't like.*

If that's not crazy, tell me what is.

Is "Just Getting by Okay"?

Money isn't a bad thing—you have to eat to live, right?—but it's not something you obsess over, either. Money is one of those things like time—it must be nice for people who have a lot of it on their hands.

I know a person who believes, "You're going to spend what you make, so just make the best of it." This is the barely-getting-by, living-paycheck-to-paycheck crowd. They're good, honest, hardworking individuals, but it seems like things are always financially tight. They have bills to pay, a mortgage to keep, and mouths to feed. They barely have money for braces, much less investments. They watch other people who've had financial success drive nice cars and live in nice houses, but they never believe they can have those things themselves.

That's the real danger with the people who have the just-getting-by mindset—believing they have little control over what happens with their money. They think you become wealthy by being born in the right family, hitting the lottery, or belonging to a secret club of elite people. This crowd doesn't realize the key to financial success isn't any of that—it simply depends on having the right attitude.

My dad used to tell me:

"Any fool can make money.
It's the wise man who holds on to it."

Don't fall for the trap of believing you don't control your money. Make wise choices and learn the truth about finances.

The Truth about Money

In *Rich Dad, Poor Dad*, Robert Kiyosaki said:

> *If you want to be rich,*
> *you need to be financially literate.*

Just like everything else in your life, your money is an area where you need to get your attitude straight and educate yourself. Managing your money is another way of managing yourself.

The average millionaire in the United States wasn't born with a silver spoon in their mouth. They're not a Wall Street trader or a famous actor. They're not some college drop-out who sold an internet company at the height of the dot-com boom. They don't have a second home on the Riviera and a third home in the Swiss Alps. They don't even drive a new car. The typical American millionaire is a first generation, self-made, self-employed businessperson who lives a seemingly average lifestyle. Wealthy people are wealthy, for the most part, because they're disciplined and smart with their money.

With money, I find the better I manage it, the more of it I seem to have. For a period of my life, I lived foolishly. I treated money like I treated time. There was always more coming, so I might as well spend it as I wanted. I didn't realize I could have been investing my money in my future. If I had saved and invested my money, I would have had a rainy day fund when the recession hit and I lost it all.

As we discussed in "Get on With It," time is something you should value, respect, and use wisely, or something you can devalue, squander, and wonder where it went. It's not that you don't have it—you make money (or you will). It's what you do with it that decides whether you enjoy success or not.

Having time isn't the point—it's what you do with it that counts. It's the exact same thing with money. Having it doesn't do you or anybody else any good. It's what you do with it that matters.

How to Attract More Money

Can we agree that, as long as you're earning money honestly and you're spending it responsibly, money is okay to have? Can we agree that, if you're a good person, you'll do good things with your money? Then can we also agree that, if you do good things with your money, having more money would let you do more good?

For me, that's the main advantage of having of money—it allows me to do good for others. I get to invest in my business and to be able to reach even more people with this message. I can pay a professional to help me with my website and marketing. I can afford to take a day off to spend with my family. I can buy my girlfriend something special for putting up with me.

For people who believe money is evil, their potential to do good is a fraction of what it could be if they would change how they think about money. If they embraced its power, maybe they could spend six months out of the year volunteering in another country. Maybe they could help launch a non-profit they believe in. Maybe they would start a business and give ten people a great job. Maybe they would donate to their local church or favorite charity. But since they believe money is bad, they push money away instead of attracting it to them.

On the flip side, people who obsess over money tend to violate some of the basic rules of business in their quest for the almighty dollar. By focusing on themselves, they see every transaction as a one-way street. The whole reason we have money in the first place is to take the place of bartering for goods and services—the equal exchange of value. When the trade only benefits one person, other people quickly learn not to do business with them. Truthfully, greedy people aren't usually successful in the long run.

People who are financially successful realize two things.

1. Like time, money is neither good nor bad, but something to be managed.

2. Money represents the value they contribute to other people's lives.

In *Relationship Selling*, author Jim Cathcart said it this way:

"Your pay will always be roughly equal to the contribution you are making. To give yourself a raise, make a greater contribution to others."

In other words, if you want to make more money, be more valuable!

People ask, "Well Ryan, what does that mean? How do I become more valuable?"

There are an endless number of ways to make yourself more valuable. You can take on more responsibility. You can be more pro-active. You can solve more problems for more people. You can learn new skills or improve your current ones. You can start a business or a non-profit and tackle bigger issues. You can contribute more time and more energy. You can be smarter and more informed. Simply being someone people like to be around makes you more valuable.

True Success

Do you remember how I defined success?

Success is being able to do what you love and get paid for it.

If you love what you do, your passion will be unmatched by anything else. You'll be the absolute best at what you do. And when you're the best at what you do, you can earn top dollar doing it. Here is another interesting quote about money and success:

People who are more interested in the work than in the money usually make more money. —Ashleigh Brilliant

I remember a phone call from a recruiter telling me about a job. It was a job I knew I would not enjoy. He said, "Do you know you can make over $100,000 doing this?"

I could, but I wouldn't be happy.

GOYA-ism:

If you don't love what you do, you're not going to be any good at it. If you love what you do, you'll be great at it.

I also take inspiration from Gary Vaynerchuk, an entrepreneur and social media guru. In his book, *Crush It!*, Gary says:

It's never a bad time to start a business unless you're starting a mediocre business.

I launched my company in the middle of the worst economy since the Great Depression. Sure, I knew times were bad—I had just lost my previous company because of it. My passion for speaking and motivating people was now

116

my new business. I was on my way to success, doing what I love. There was no way that I was going to let this be a mediocre business.

Do Good for Yourself and Others

Use your money to do good for others.

I'll never forget the time I was walking back to my car after a social event and a man stopped me to ask for some money. He said he had lost his job and had a family to feed. Instead of giving him money, I told him to hop in the car. I took him to a nearby grocery store and told him to get whatever he needed while I waited at the front.

After about fifteen minutes, he came back with the normal stuff—milk, bread, sandwich meat, a two-liter Coke, and couple of other things. Together, it all cost about thirty dollars. Outside the store, the man threw his arms around me and started crying. You would have thought I had given him a million dollars! He didn't know it, but I gained more out of that exchange than he did.

When you focus on helping others and adding value to their lives, you'll see more value added to yours. As you make money, remember to spend it wisely, just as you spend your time. Invest it in yourself, in your family, in your community, and in your dreams. Money is just a measure of value. The more money you have, the more you can trade it for the things that are truly valuable in life.

Make money. Do good. End of story.

GOYA-cise:

Do a monthly budget and track exactly how you spend your money. Make a wish list of all the good things you would do if you had money to spare. Find one worthy cause and give regularly, even if it's just a dollar a week.

Even though I've talked about how your attitude and life affects other people, everything we've covered up to this point has really been about you. Even in "Soar With the Eagles," the focus was on how positive relationships affect your life. The next two chapters deal with the rest of life—your attitude toward other people.

Chapter 10

SAY THANK YOU

Of all the "attitudes" we can acquire, surely the attitude of gratitude is the most important and by far the most life-changing. —Zig Ziglar

C AN YOU IMAGINE BEING GRATEFUL you were fired? Do you think you'd be happy if your significant other broke up with you? Can you picture yourself getting shot and saying, "Thank You!"?

I can't pretend I was immediately thankful when all those things happened to me, but looking back I'm glad they did. I'm grateful for the misfortune and the challenges I've had in my life because they've made me a much better person. Losing one of my first sales jobs made me go out and find a better one, and motivated me to go finish my degree and do my best at every job after that one. I didn't ever want to be fired again.

I'm glad an old girlfriend broke up with me. I realized later she wasn't the right one for me.

Getting shot opened my eyes to the importance of health and prompted me to enroll in sports medicine at the University of Southern Mississippi. I made some lifelong friends, had a great time in college, and learned healthy habits that will stay with me for the rest of my life.

There's a reason everything happens. If you panic or focus on an immediate crisis, you'll miss the chance to let it make you stronger. But if you adopt Zig Ziglar's "attitude of gratitude," you'll start with the mindset of, "I'm okay with what just happened. I'm grateful I have the opportunity to grow."

What about you? Have you reached the point that you can be grateful for what's happened in your past? Was it someone who did something to you? Was it no one's fault—just something that happened by accident? Was it something you did to yourself?

Being thankful for what happened takes a lot of time and maturity. It took me a long time to have the outlook I have now with a lot of prayer, effort, and soul-searching. If you're not there yet, I promise you this—it's worth it.

Everyday Thanks

But an attitude of gratitude isn't just about the big things in life. It's a daily habit—really almost a lifestyle.

Say Thank You

A thankful spirit is inherently a positive one. When you go around saying "thank you" all the time, it cultivates a mindset that's focused on all the great things in life around you. The more you're thankful for, the more you'll find to be thankful for.

When the girl at the cash register is handing you your change, look her in the eye and say "thank you." She could have been incompetent. She could have had a horrible demeanor. She could have been rude. But she wasn't. She was just doing her job. When you say thank you, you're telling her you're grateful she made the choice not to spoil your day.

People are taken aback when you say "thank you" and really mean it. It's just two simple words, but we've gotten so caught up in our own lives and worries that we've forgotten how to express an idea we learned as children.

For some reason, it seems like we've raised the bar on what it takes to elicit a "thank you" from someone. You don't get acknowledged because you're doing what you're supposed to. You only get recognition if you go far and beyond the call of duty to help someone out.

People don't care how much you know until they know how much you care. —John Maxwell

People love being around people they know care about them. As human beings, we love feeling that we've helped someone or did something worthy of a "thank you." My nephew, Dakota, always says "thank you." Even if I do something as easy as pouring him a Coke, he'll say "Thank you." It's notable and memorable because it's so rare—and it makes me want to do more for him because I know he appreciates it.

One of the best and most important business lessons I ever learned was to write thank-you notes. They're inexpensive but worth an incredible amount. Whether you're in business or not, get into the habit of dashing off quick thank-you cards as a way of expressing your gratitude to someone. I really don't understand why something so simple and yet so appreciated is so uncommon.

Start saying "thank you" to everyone who does anything for you and watch how much they appreciate it. Notice how much better you feel.

Realize What You Have

Don't wait to give thanks until someone has done something worth the thanks. Get your mind off the immediate and see the big picture. Thank people for just being who they are. Call your parents or your grandparents for no reason and thank them for loving you.

I'll never forget the day I lost my grandmother. I was in the eighth grade. I was supposed to go to her house that weekend, but I decided to stay home with my brothers and sister. My parents had gone to an antique auction and left my older brother to watch us.

Earlier that day, my grandmother called to talk to me. She just wanted to see how I was doing and when I was going to come see her. I told her I was sorry I didn't come that weekend, but I would come see her soon. I told her I loved her and we hung up. That was the last time we talked. That evening, someone broke into her house and she suffered a fatal heart attack.

For years I carried the guilt of wishing I had been there for her. Maybe I could have prevented what happened or helped her somehow. I don't know. I've always regretted that I never had the chance to tell her how much she really meant to me, how much I loved her, and how much I owed her.

If there's someone like that in your life, make sure you thank them every chance you get.

Sometimes you don't know how to be grateful for something until it's gone.

Everyone's heard about the devastation of Hurricane Katrina. It was very personal for me. When Katrina hit, I was living in Dallas. One of my best friends, Tim, and I immediately loaded our vehicle with water and gas and drove to our hometown of Slidell, Louisiana, (a suburb north of New Orleans). We didn't know what to expect. I hadn't heard from my family since the hurricane struck. Telephone land lines were down and cell phone towers were destroyed. I had no idea if they were okay or not.

When we arrived, I found my brother and then found the rest of my family. Thank God none of them were hurt physically. The devastation was incredible. It was like a war zone we see on television in a third world country. There was no running water, no utilities, no power, no stores open.

It made me realize how thankful I should be for the big things in life—like my family being okay—and helped me be thankful for the little things in life, like running water and being able to run down to the store for a loaf of bread.

Try to notice the things you take for granted—the little things and the big things—and remember to feel grateful for them.

GOYA-ism:

Never compare what you don't have to what others have.
Appreciate what you do have!

Live Gratefully

Sometimes it's not enough to simply say "thanks." You need to live gratefully. How do you do it?

Say Thank You

As we express our gratitude, we must never forget that the highest appreciation is not to utter words, but to live by them. —John F. Kennedy

If you are a business owner, you should be grateful for the people who work for you. You're not doing them a favor by employing them—they're doing you a favor by working for you. They can hang up their apron or tool belt and go home today; you're the one who needs them to keep working and making money. It's your name on the building and your signature on the loan.

If you're an employee, don't look at customers as problems to be handled. The reality is your boss doesn't pay you—your paycheck actually comes from the customer.

If you're a teenager, think about this: A friend of mine administered a home for pregnant and parenting teen girls. Many of those girls had parents and family who could have taken care of them, but they chose not to. If you have a parent who makes sure you have food, clothes, and a bed at night, be thankful.

If you have tragically lost a loved one like I did, be thankful you have some good memories. My grandmother was the only grandparent I knew. I didn't have the chance to know my other grandparents. If you know yours, be thankful.

Life is too short to be wrapped up in yourself and your disappointments all the time. Start saying "thank you" for everyone and everything in your life.

Live gratefully and you'll live well!

GOYA-cise:

Any time you're feeling down, start listing all the things you have to be grateful for. Each morning, quickly run down your list and add new things. For the next 24 hours, say "thank you" to everyone you see and notice their reaction. Go buy a pack of thank-you notes and use them every chance you get.

Saying "thank you" reminds you to be grateful—to take the focus off of your own life and thank other people for what they're doing with their life. But don't just express gratitude—live a life of gratitude by being someone's miracle.

Chapter 11

BE SOMEONE'S MIRACLE

Every day holds the possibility of a miracle.
—Elizabeth David

THERE'S A GIRL FROM my hometown, who has one of the most inspiring stories I've ever heard. Ashlee Stokes was fifteen years old when she was hit by a drunk driver. After weeks in a coma, she finally woke up, but the damage had been severe.

Out of all this, do you know what she asked her father for? She asked him if he would start a free pick-up service for people who had had too much to drink. Ashlee had already come up with the slogan for the organization: *Swallow your pride and call for a ride.*

This little girl hadn't even recovered from her terrible tragedy when she became a miracle to countless people. Who knows how many accidents Ashlee's Angels have prevented, how many lives have been saved, and how many futures have remained bright?

GOYA-ism:

Sometimes, you're waiting on a miracle.
Sometimes, the miracle is waiting on you.

A great postscript to this story is that her schoolmates elected her homecoming queen and she has gone on to graduate high school.

Give Back

What is a miracle? It's getting past yourself and giving back to the world. It's taking the spotlight off of you and shining it on someone else. It's realizing that life is not always about you.

I wonder where I would be if wonderful people hadn't helped me when I needed it. What would my life be like if teachers, family, friends, co-workers, and mentors hadn't helped me? What if no one had reached back to pull me forward?

You have to remember that whatever you achieve in life isn't accomplished by yourself. An African proverb says it takes a village to raise a child. In other words, part of who you are comes from the positive influence of those around you. You didn't arrive here by yourself. It's your *eagles* who got you where you are.

How do you give? You can give in ways that you'll remember for the rest of your life or in ways that you might forget next week.

Too many people have what I call "Little Ant Syndrome." They see themselves as tiny ants on a huge planet. What difference can one person possibly make?

GOYA-ism:

You may not change the entire world, but you can change someone else's world by being their miracle.

You can make a difference!

Have you ever noticed that when you focus on someone else's problem, your problems don't seem to be so bad?

When a series of horrific tornadoes cut through the south, one news report showed a victim whose house had been destroyed. The amazing thing was, she was in her Red Cross uniform, helping others at a shelter.

That's the miracle—people living not only for themselves but also for others.

What's your attitude toward helping others? Are you one of those every-man-for-himself types? Or do you believe service is not only your privilege but your responsibility?

Think back over the past month. What have you done to help someone else?

Miracles Come in All Shapes and Sizes

My older brother, my brother-in-law, and my oldest nephew are all firefighters. They don't do it because they can't get another job or because they'll one day make millions. They don't do it because they're adrenaline junkies and enjoy the rush of danger. They do it because they've devoted their career and their lives to saving others.

They're everyday heroes.

Miracles can come in very small packages, too. One of my mentors, after hearing me speak, told me I was a very talented speaker. It didn't take him five seconds to say that, but it's something that will stay with me for the rest of my life. You can be a mentor—you can whisper words of hope, life, and encouragement into someone's ear.

Everyone has some kind of skill, expertise, or talent. That's a perfect way to give back. After the devastating earthquake in Haiti, Dr. Craig Greene, a doctor I met at church, flew to the island to lend his medical skills. Writing a check to the American Red Cross would have been easier, but his expertise was what was needed. He worked twelve-to-fourteen-hour days to help the earthquake victims and the overwhelmed hospitals.

His example inspired me to take inventory of my skills. What unique abilities do I have to give back?

Speaking is my gift. I sometimes work with schools and worthy causes to help them advance their missions. I didn't write this book to see my name on a shelf in a bookstore. That's not to say it's not exciting, but I felt inspired to write it in the hope it would help others to get off their attitude—to realize the negativity that was holding them back from their potential, and from the fulfilling positive life they could be living. I think what I'm doing with my business is, in part, one of the ways I can give back.

Another way I give back is with my *Get Off Your Attitude* bracelet. Every time one sells, a portion of the proceeds goes to a worthy cause. I'm fortunate to have the opportunity to return, in a small way, the help and support I've been given.

In working with worthy causes, I had the chance to work with Darryn and Cherine DeWalt, the marketing agents for New Orleans Saints player Darren Sharper. They started the "Get Checked or Check Out!" organization to promote healthy initiatives and habits in targeted communities. This is what floored me: They started the foundation even while he was battling a rare form of cancer.

It's easier to be a miracle when everything is going right in your life. However, Ashlee, the Dewalts and the Red Cross volunteer, took the focus off of their needs and shined the light on others' needs. They were helping others even while they needed a miracle themselves.

When I tell you to surround yourself with positive people and collect inspiring stories, these are the people I'm talking about: Friends and mentors who will whisper words of hope; everyday heroes who put their lives on the line for others; and people who want to help others even though they have every right to focus on themselves.

Find people like these to inspire you. When you come across a story that tugs at your heart, cut it out or print it. Make a scrapbook of these heroes. Let the miracles they give inspire you to give your own.

How Do You Give Back?

You can be someone's miracle. All it takes is the right attitude. Whenever you find someone with a bigger problem than yours, become their miracle. While you are becoming their miracle, they may become yours.

The miracle you make could be as simple as listening to someone. I recently read an article which said the suicide rate in our region was up. I wonder how many of those people simply needed someone who would not only talk with them, but also listen to them. How many lives could have been saved by knowing someone cared enough to spend a few hours listening?

You can lend an ear or lend a hand. There are thousands of non-profit and volunteer organizations who desperately need your help. They're looking for someone who can pack food boxes, stuff envelopes, or staff a booth at a fundraising event. You don't need some special talent to do any of that and you can still make a difference!

GOYA-ism:

Every day can be a miracle if you decide to make it one.

What talents and skills you do have? Take an inventory of yourself. Are you an accountant? Plenty of people and organizations need help managing their finances. Are you a college student? Your age could help you connect with a high school student struggling in a subject related to your major. Are you a mechanic? I'm sure you wouldn't have to look very far to find deserving people who can't afford to fix their car.

Are you retired? Do you know how many children would love to have a grandparent-like figure in their lives? Whoever you are, you have the time, the resources, and the talents to be someone's miracle.

I encourage you to start there and then go even further. I hope your entire life becomes a miracle to others. I hope you find your purpose and then pursue it with everything you have. I would love to see you become an inspiration to the entire world.

GOYA-cise:

Commit to donating your time to a worthy cause on a regular basis. Find an opportunity every day to inspire hope and to be someone's miracle, even when you are having a bad day. Make a scrapbook of other miracles you've seen or experienced. Use them for inspiration.

The last chapter of this book is about taking everything you've read so far and putting it into action.

My friend Gary Borgstede, author of *The Make it Happen Journey*, once shared this with me:

"Make it happen people possess a positive 'make it happen' attitude."

It's time to get off your attitude and make it happen!

Chapter 12

MAKE IT HAPPEN!

Y OU HAVE THE POWER to change your habits, your
life, and your destiny. It starts with the positive
choice to get off your attitude.

Let's review the definition of "Get Off Your Attitude."

It means:

• To think positive and take action;
• To talk, believe, act, and think in a positive manner;
• To create a positive mindset during a negative situation or environment;
• To help someone to create a positive mindset to overcome fear, adversity, oppression, or challenges that person may face in life.

Where do you start? Begin by taking responsibility for your own life. Get serious.

It's up to you. If you want to change your life, change your attitude.

Don't blame your parents, your past, or anything else. Point the finger at yourself. This is your life, right now. What are you going to do about it?

It's as simple as this: You have two options. You can sit around complaining or you can get off your attitude and make it happen!

Invest in Yourself!

Your life is not only a lifelong project—it's a lifelong *learning* project. Approach it that way and you'll always be developing better, smarter habits. The problem is most people work harder on their jobs than they do on themselves. What do I mean by that?

My junior year of college I quit the University of Southern Mississippi to move to Dallas and start my career. After a year or so, I was on my way to making a good income. I was doing well for a college dropout! Yet, I was confused about my future. I knew I wanted to go back to college and finish, but wasn't quite sure when or how I should. I was told by my manager that I would never move up in the company without a degree.

Soon after that, I was talking to a close friend who said, "Ryan, you need to go back and finish your degree."

This was coming from a guy who was very successful, had a degree, and was well-respected in his field.

It was a hard decision for me to make. In the end, I realized it was the best thing to do and took his advice. I moved to Baton Rouge. It wasn't easy to go from a guaranteed base salary plus commission to waiting tables. However, I knew finishing my education was what I needed to do. And that's what I did. I earned my bachelor's degree in marketing at Southeastern Louisiana University.

I thought my education was over the day I graduated. I discovered I was dead wrong. That was the day it began.

Formal education will make you a living. Self-education will make you a fortune. —Jim Rohn

Although I returned to Dallas after graduation, I didn't truly enjoy my career until I began to invest in my self-education. That is when I learned you don't *chase* money—you *attract* it by becoming better in your personal and professional life. I attended seminars, listened to CDs, and read business and self-development books. I was doing it so I could be better in my career; so I could be better in life, and become a better person overall.

Maybe you're like I was—totally unfamiliar with self-development. I didn't realize there was that much great information out there to help you improve yourself.

If you don't like reading books, I can empathize. When I got out of college, I was so sick of reading that I never wanted to see another book. I told one of my mentors about my negative attitude toward reading and he immediately asked me, "Do you know how to eat an elephant?" I had no idea what he meant. He then told me "One bite at a time." Then he explained that's the same way you read a book… just a chapter a day.

Books are one way to go, but you can invest in yourself in a lot of other ways. I enjoy watching shows such as, *A & E's Biography,* VH1's *Behind the Music,* and ESPN's *Beyond the Glory.* These series take you behind the scenes to show you the hardships that celebrities, entrepreneurs, athletes, and other professionals had to face in pursuing their dreams. I'm energized at the end of each episode— feeling that I could take on anything, and thinking, if they can do it, so can I!

Other great resources I love are CD sets, audio books, and podcasts. You can listen to these while you drive, exercise, or during many other activities. Attending seminars are another incredible way to pick up new ideas. You can find many excellent seminars through an internet search or by calling a professional organization.

You have the same opportunities. If you have basic internet access, you can read, watch, or listen to inspiring stories and find personal development resources. The number one excuse I hear is, "I don't have the time." If you listen to the radio, you can listen to a CD. If you read a forwarded chain email, you can read an uplifting story. If you're watching television, watch something positive, such as *Biography*.

You have the time and opportunity. What it takes is committing to making yourself better. Stay away from all the negativity, because it will creep into your subconscious and become part of your everyday life! Remember— positive in, positive out.

That's what it means to work on yourself. You have to be constantly investing in your own development and exposing yourself to new ideas and experiences. You need to be inspired by other people and stories. Learning, reading, and growing are part of your positive attitude strategy.

Some say knowledge is power, but I believe *applied knowledge* is power. There's no advantage in knowing something and never using it. Go learn it—then go do it!

GOYA-ism:

Look at yourself as a lifelong project that you're always trying to make better.

Adopt a Winning Attitude!

My nephew Dakota has the winning attitude I'm talking about. At sixty pounds and 4 feet 3 inches, he doesn't look like your typical youth football player. His teammates named him "Mini-Me." A lot of people would look at him and say he doesn't have what it takes—but last year, Mini-Me took home the award for having the biggest heart and the most courage. His coach told me he wishes every one of his players had Dakota's drive and commitment. He puts 110 percent in every game and isn't scared to take on kids twice his size.

You have to have that same drive! You'll never achieve your dreams and change your life until you start believing you can. Don't sit there and let life pass you by. Get out there and win!

Let's recap the following habits you need to develop in order to adopt that winning attitude:

1. Think, talk, and act positive. Start with the choice to be positive in every area of your life. Develop the habit of thinking, talking, and acting with optimism in every situation. Regardless of what happens in life, you have the power to choose your response. Your response will reflect your attitude, and your attitude will determine your future.

2. Engage in positive relationships. Your mind is a magnet, subconsciously picking up everything around it. You can't soar with the eagles during the day if you're bumming around with the owls at night. Find others who will encourage you and lift you higher. Surround yourself with great people, and it won't be long until you're an eagle also!

3. Passionately pursue your purpose. Whatever your dream is, go after it! Everyone has a dream. Maybe yours has been buried so long you've forgotten about it—but it's never too late to start! The only question about reaching your dreams is this: How badly do you want it?

4. Live in the now. Fully engage the present. This moment—right now—is all the time you have. Spend your time on what matters most and where it will improve your life. Respect what time you have left and make the most of it!

5. Forgive and forget. Don't let your past define your future. Come to peace with whatever you've done to yourself or what others have done to you. Accept the fact that you can't change it. Trying to relive yesterday only robs you of enjoying your life today and the shaping of your tomorrow. You have your whole life ahead of you. Do something great with it.

6. Smile! Welcome adversity as an opportunity to grow. If you'll smile, figuratively and literally, you'll overcome the challenges of daily life and use them as stepping stones to your success. Look adversity in the face—and SMILE!

7. Be courageous. No one can see the future. You can't wait until you know everything will turn out all right before you act. Be confident in your spiritual faith, in yourself, and in others—especially

when you don't have a reason for that confidence. Stay aligned with your calling. Keep the faith!

8. Take care of yourself. Your physical health and mental health go hand in hand. It's hard to have one without the other. Exercise, eat right, sleep right, and adopt a positive attitude about your body. The more you take care of your body, the more it will take care of you!

9. Do good. Money is like time—what you do with it is the important thing. Get your attitude toward money straight. It's nothing to be greedy over or ashamed of. Learn to attract money, and then use it to do good for yourself and others.

10. Be grateful. Say "thank you." Appreciate those who have invested in your life, who do big and little things for you, and who have influenced you for the better. Adopt an attitude of gratitude. Be thankful for everyone and everything in your life.

11. Give back. Find ways to help others, making this a better world. Take the spotlight off of yourself and shine it on others. You have the time, talents, and resources to do something amazing. Be a miracle.

12. Make it happen! Take responsibility to change your life for the better. Commit, sacrifice, and discipline yourself to making a positive change in your life. Invest in yourself through personal and formal education. It's your decision. It's your destiny!

As you focus on what you're achieving, don't neglect how you're achieving it. Be a person of character. Be honest. Be trustworthy. Have a reputation of the absolute highest integrity. Do things for the all the right reasons and not the wrong ones. Keep a humble spirit. Always be grateful.

Blaze a Trail

As you begin to develop these habits and to make positive choices in your life, you will become the person you want to be. As you create a positive lifestyle, you're blazing a trail for others. You're setting an example for the people around you of what's possible. You're becoming a leader.

A leader isn't the person in charge—it's the person other people are following. You may not think of yourself as a leader. Maybe you don't even want to be one. Don't focus on that. Work on becoming positive in how you think, talk, and act in every area of your life. Simply by doing that, you're paving the way for other people to walk that same path. By being better, you're inspiring other people to be better, too!

Leave a Legacy

I never had the opportunity to really know my grand-father. One day while rummaging through an old trunk of his, I found this inspiring message. Out of all the things my grandfather could have passed on to his grandson, I think this message—misspellings and all—was the best thing he could have left:

"Its What You Go After in Life"

The expression of a person's life comes about as the result of what he has gone out into the world to gain.

If a person looks to others for the carrying of his burdens and for the solving of his problems, only weakness and unhappiness are invited. It's what you go after on your own account that gives you health, respect, and a feeling of power.

Even the one who fails at doing something may ultimately find success. All too often some men and women seem to need the continual beating of failure at their doors to adequately arm themselves for a substantial success. The veteran knows more about defeat and retreats than he does about victories.

It all depends upon what you want, what you have in the secret chamber of your mind and heart as the ultimate destination of your life, and your measure of success and happiness in this life.

You will be in happiness large what you are daily going after in your mind and heart and with your hands...

Never mind what others think! It is what you think, what you plan, what you dream, what you know you are capable of achieving that is going to count. Nothing else matters.

—George Madison Adams

Make It Happen!

Whenever I start to doubt myself, I go to that tattered piece of yellowing paper, which is now framed and hanging in my office, and read the last paragraph again:

"Never mind what others think! It is what you think, what you plan, what you dream, what you know you are capable of achieving that is going to count. Nothing else matters."

Reading it helps me change my attitude. It reminds me that when I am going after my dreams, it's what I think, what I plan, and my ability to make it happen that counts.

I am very grateful for those dreams that I have been able to achieve. However, this isn't the end of my journey. It's just the beginning! I want to write more books, develop more educational products, and continue speaking at seminars. I also plan to start the Get Off Your Attitude Foundation to help others.

I hope the dreams that I have achieved and those that I passionately pursue will become my legacy to generations to come. I hope I've inspired you to live a positive lifestyle and to go after your dreams. When you achieve them, don't stop there! Leave a legacy that you will be proud of.

Make sure the last chapter of your book will say that you were a loving, encouraging, and inspiring person. I hope that it will say that you were also a friend, mentor, giver, and that you passionately pursued your dreams... and achieved them!

Make it happen!

Get off your attitude!

MEET THE AUTHOR

Ryan C. Lowe
Speaker. Coach. Consultant
Motivation – Workshop – Keynote

Ryan Lowe is a motivational speaker, coach, and consultant. He has delivered presentations to companies of all sizes, from small businesses to Fortune 500s, resulting in higher performance in individuals and organizations. More importantly, he has inspired people throughout the country to have a positive attitude and achieve their professional and personal goals by sharing his own experiences in dealing with adversity.

147

During his career Ryan has achieved award-winning sales positions and became one of the most-requested speakers/trainers with Brian Tracy Seminars, The American Sales Trainer Association, Universal Seminars, and The Productivity People. He has also served as the vice-president of sales for two financial services corporations and as a partner in a financial services start-up. He has presented to sales groups, financial institutions, churches, sports groups, non-profits, schools, civic organizations, and more.

Ryan's life story, wealth of professional experience, and incredible delivery make him one of the best-loved and most sought-after motivational speakers today. Having survived several personal tragedies including a near-death experience, he's on a mission. He's spreading his positive attitude message: Success isn't determined by background, experience, or anything else. It's all in your attitude. In his seminars and his own life, Ryan inspires people to believe they, too, can "get off their attitude" and achieve the life they've envisioned.

After living in many cities across the country, Ryan now resides in Mandeville, Louisiana, where he is close to his family and his New Orleans roots.